FOREWORD

Fly fishing for Pacific salmon is primarily done in rivers. Throughout their original distribution from Alaska to California, anglers have pursued them. In the rivers of northern California and southern Oregon where fly fishing for salmon has been practiced diligently for about four decades, dedicated anglers unfailingly return each autumn hoping to meet schools of salmon as they return from their long ocean journeys. It is the intention of these anglers to catch salmon in the estuary pools as close to the ocean as possible when the fish are still "bright."

Sometimes carrying sea lice and still looking very much like ocean residents, the silvery sides of these salmon do not reveal the dramatic, biological change already taking place. In the last stage of their saline lives, they fed heavily to prepare for their long and final ordeal. But for many of these salmon, by the time they reach freshwater, their digestive tracts have begun to

shrivel. At this stage the only part of their system still developing are the reproductive organs that must produce eggs and sperm for their final act.

There is no argument that while en route to their final destination Pacific salmon, especially the king or Chinook, the largest of the family, are formidable opponents when hooked with fly tackle. Without bringing up the issue of whether it is sporting to pursue fish that are past their prime, I suspect that every serious salmon fly fisher is curious about the fighting quality of salmon caught at sea compared to that of the same fish caught in a river. In rivers, Pacific salmon are schooled and vulnerable and while they definitely do not feed, they will "taste" items that drift with the current or lie on the stream bottom. This tasting is a natural behavior for salmon as it reinforces their unerring route of return to the waters in which they were born.

The lengths to which salmon will go to "taste" objects was made clear to me long before I fished for them with flies. Besides using bait, I also fished for salmon with lures. Once while using spoons on a short coastal river in northern California, I made a poor cast and ended up with the cursed back-lash. While untangling the mess my spoon sat on the bottom. After straightening the line on the spool, and before winding the line taut to retrieve the spoon, the line tightened on its own. The next thing I knew, I was connected to a nice coho that had picked the spoon off the bottom and hooked itself.

Anglers who had caught salmon in saltwater told me that coho stage in the saltwater bay before entering the stream. This sounded like an interesting opportunity so I made plans to pursue them "outside." To have a chance for these salmon, a boat was needed and since I was committed entirely to fishing I had a suitable one. What I didn't have, though, was any idea how to catch salmon once out there.

In time I learned about tidal influences and the most likely places salmon would gather, and the first one I hooked in saltwater on a spoon was a real eye opener. This fish moved with greater speed than any river silver I had ever hooked. The line hissed as it cut a sharp slice through the water behind the quick moving fish. My bait casting reel seemed motorized as the level wind raced back and forth. Some quick aerobatics and the fish was off again, totally out of my control until, finally, it jumped and tossed the hook. That wild contest lasted less than thirty seconds! I couldn't believe these fish were the same species found in freshwater. I called them rocket fish.

That episode with lures took place more than twenty years ago, but to this day I've only taken a handful of salmon with a cast fly in saltwater. None of these catches have been notable and most were chum salmon. The only king I've landed was not much bigger than a large sea-run cutthroat, the fish I was after at the time. In fact, I first thought it was a cutthroat until I noticed its black, inner mouth.

I have come close to hooking some large kings on a cast fly in the ocean... They've followed my flies with their noses almost touching the feathers. Some even swirled so near my fly that I struck thinking my offering had been taken. But the worst thing was that after refusing to take my fly, they would jump on a mooched anchovy or hit a lure without any hesitation. Even if I had been more persistent and more determined to catch a mature salmon in saltwater on a cast fly, there is still no guarantee I would have prevailed. The mystery for me remains.

If my attempts to catch salmon in the open ocean on a cast fly were made on more fertile grounds, maybe the results would have been different. Most of my trips have been in the ocean off central California, a place where salmon have only lately been protected from commercial fishing. While it is said there are early signs that depressed stocks are rebounding here, in the last quarter century Pacific salmon everywhere have dwindled far more rapidly than anyone could have predicted, and the genetic integrity of the few remaining wild stocks is being severely attacked by hatchery mentality. Even worse, special interest groups are so well established and influential that their lawyers argue in court whether less than 200 salmon of one kind entitles these fish to be considered endangered! This is exactly the case for the winter-run king salmon of the Sacramento River in California.

My own observations on a recent trip for steelhead on the Salmon River in Idaho with my wife Chris to gather information for our newsletter *The Inside Angler* also sums up what is happening. We were successful in catching steelhead, but virtually all of them were hatchery-reared. And if that wasn't bad enough, we learned the fish for which this famous river was named are just about extinct. When and how will the downward spiral of Pacific salmon be reversed?

Unless more effective measures are taken to preserve wild stocks of salmon, the future is not bright for these fish. Our population continues to grow and with it comes domestic and industrial pollution, declining water quality, resource degradation, and steadily disappearing wildlife. Genetic diversity of species is sacrificed and life forms are homogenized to accommodate human expansion. This biological suicide is ripe for invasion by ever-evolving diseases that weaken and destroy the last remaining pure strains of salmon left on the west coast.

It is in this climate that Jim Crawford writes about catching Pacific salmon on a cast fly in saltwater. It is a challenge met by only a rare few. As you read this fine, well crafted and well researched book, I believe you will appreciate this adventure in angling and the fact that the spirit that kindles it still lives on. *Salmon to a Fly* concerns innovative fishing in its purist form. No one before has had the resources or invested the time required for this pursuit and then written about it. We are truly privileged that Jim shares his knowledge and experience. Personally, this book will go a long way in helping me catch a mature salmon on a cast fly in the open ocean...and it will provide answers to other fly fishers in my predicament as well.

Michael Fong
San Francisco, California
March, 1995

INTRODUCTION

Trying to fly fish every piece of water that you hear is great for salmon along the west coast is an absurd impossibility...yet from the vast emptiness that sometimes is my mind comes a strange urge to try. The ocean holds a powerful, almost mystical attraction for me and I know, as surely as does any addict, that the very next attempt will yield success so spectacular I won't even have to lie about it! So I go, eyes glazed, to find *that* place.

Last year I found it at the northern tip of Queen Charlotte Islands, a region that looks so primitive and untouched it was easy to fantasize I was the first to ever cast a fly there. More absurdity I know, but the fishing is *so* incredible. Three of the five Pacific salmon came to my patterns (yes, there *are* six, but masu salmon from Asia and Russia don't get over here too often)—seven Chinooks, more coho, and a hoard of pinks. And one halibut offered itself on a wildly windy boat-pitching day that had stopped being fun as soon the northwester roared in from somewhere out towards Japan. Success? Yes. Sick? Almost. Will I go back? Absolutely.

Another time I found it along the mysterious outer coast of Vancouver Island with two close friends. A thick coating of logging road dust covered everything—boat, equipment, sleeping bags, food—and swirled up our noses and into our ears and eyes as we raced the nine miles across little-known waters to Kyuquot and our island camp. But we were each too preoccupied with our own personal agendas to notice. Huge salmon would come to our unique fishing techniques over the next week, and even relentless winds and penetratingly cold, thick, gray fog wouldn't change our rose-colored outlook. It did get us lost a time or two, but that didn't matter. At night, warming to a glowing fire and good scotch, we would hear the songs and drums of the ancient Nootka people on the soft winds of time. Success is measured in many ways.

Still another time I discovered it outside the immense kelp bed that protects the bay at Pillar Point on Juan De Fuca Strait. My thoughts were in the ozone when the Chinook came out from the fronds, gently took my fly and returned to the sanctuary of its watery maze. I didn't comprehend until it breached somewhere deep inside the tangle. A bald eagle watched my quandary for a while, then soared away to find a more promising outcome.

I'd like to say I landed that fish but the eagle knew... Still, it was a monumental achievement. That Chinook was the first I ever hooked on a cast fly in the ocean.

Other ventures I'll describe have also yielded outstanding successes, and certainly just as many weren't so giving. Some of those will be mentioned too because frequently defeats are exhilaratingly memorable. I have had the great fortune to fish with friends for salmon in the open ocean from California to Alaska, and while the destinations in this book are limited to British Columbia because of space and familiarity, the methods and techniques described can be applied to waters all along the west coast where similar conditions are encountered.

Equipment, tackle, patterns, techniques, methods—all are discussed as they apply to various encounters. And while some rods and reels and lines are mentioned by brand name, that doesn't mean those specific labels are "required" for success. The only one constant is—and it's assumed anyone intending to fish in the ocean knows this—tackle must be suitable for use in saltwater.

The sum and substance of fly fishing the open Pacific is to face the true spirit of nature, at times generous and mild and at other times heartless and ill-tempered. The ocean is not for the timid or overconfident. It can take you whenever it wants. But those who go there to connect with nature can embrace the opportunity to rethink values and priorities, and almost surely come away with greater respect for the sea and shame for what we are doing to it and the land that cradles and nurtures it.

Western coastal forests and rivers are devastated beyond comprehension. Hundreds of once-fine salmonid spawning streams are now silted and clogged with debris, strangled by the profound power of bottom line culture. Intangibles such as wilderness, biodiversity and scenic value do not sit well with corporations intent on profit or bureaucrats with specific political agendas. The thought of what it must have been like causes me to point my less-than-perfect finger at government, dam builders, and the forest and mining industries for doing everything possible to violate nature's soul. Yet I too am guilty for what has been lost. I wanted things development brought and took what nature gave, and I justify my past abuses by whining *everyone did it*.

Now my generation writes books and stories about how much more aware we are of the consequences of irresponsible actions and proclaim we will make it better. Today trees still fall, streams still smother, dams still dam, seiners, trollers, gill-netters, and sport fishers still fish...and salmon continue to die. The process is endless. Every user group blames the other and feels righteous in its reason. Somewhere it must stop!

And so I write this to tell how to catch salmon in the last remaining place they have that hasn't quite been destroyed. I can't keep it a secret! Somewhere I read that if we don't tell then no one will know it's worth saving. Sounds reasonable. As fly fishers we are the true guardians—the last hope— of the future of salmonids. What we show others through our natural instinct to be conservators by catch-and-release and by speaking out against the degradation of our environment and by becoming involved through organizations like The Nature Conservancy, the Federation of Fly Fishers and its member clubs and other groups, will help. So go to the places you'll read about in this book. Discover your own, too. And in your remorse release one for me and spread the word that these places and their gifts deserve to endure forever.

Maybe trying to fish all the last, best Pacific coast salmon places isn't as absurd as it seems.

TRANSITION

Sacramento, Feather, Eel, Smith, Chetco... Without question I would still be thrashing some of these rivers for salmon, chasing the dreams legends like Bill Schaadt, Bob Nauheim, Dan Blanton, Russ Chatham and others weaved with their fly rods during my "earlier" impressionistic days, except that in 1968 I moved to British Columbia where at the very least it is immoral—if not illegal—to actively pursue salmon once they have entered their home rivers to spawn.

"But we catch-and-release in rivers," you say, "we don't hurt the fish. Besides, what's the difference if a salmon is caught in a river or the ocean..."

Fair comments, but let me relate a quick contrition I wrote after being away from river salmon a few years. It accounts for my present philosophy and perhaps will strike a supportive chord or two out there.

CONTAMINATION OF A FLY FISHER

The 135 miles of US 101 from Reedsport to our destination at Brookings clings for most of its distance to the often rugged, sometimes sand-duned, always beautiful Oregon coastline and crosses rivers bearing names that conjure visions: Umpqua, Coos, Coquille, Sixes, Rogue, Pistol, Elk, Chetco...

It was sometime in November 1982 and my first trip to fish Chinooks in moving water since leaving California in 1968 to live in British Columbia. I still had a couple of Pflueger fly reels with lead-core shooting tapers and monofilament backing that I bought during my "low-economy" university days to use for salmon on rivers like the Eel and Smith and for shad on the Yuba. The only equipment change was a new graphite rod to replace my old Fenwick FF98 that had been faithful for more years than I care to admit.

The Chetco is perhaps Oregon's finest salmon and steelhead river...a statement that may surprise even some Oregonians. Comparatively short—about 28 fishable miles—the Chetco's upper watershed had been spared the ravages of heavy logging. Beautifully clear and clean it cuts through steep, treed hills and around rugged rock outcrops to form deep holding pools and long sliding runs. For the next week I was to become intimate with salmon in Loeb Pool, Willow Hole, Pilings Run, Tamba, Rip-Rap, Hiway Hole, Social Security, Tide Rock, Morrison... More places than can be thoroughly fished in the week we would be there.

Being the "rookie" in the group I was assigned the Loeb drift beginning about eight miles upriver from where the Chetco meets saltwater. Fifty-one Chinooks to 57 pounds were netted by fisheries officials only the day before in the two Loeb Park pools. They would be kept alive in holding tanks at a nearby hatchery for stripping to supplement low returns in other rivers. Netting that many in only a couple of passes meant there would be many more fish still holding, so it was a top spot.

Loeb Pool is perhaps two hundred feet long and a hundred feet wide, a deep brooding hole tucked against a steep rock bank and always in shade. That day it held between 200 and 300 salmon, and we could see some were monsters. Chinooks in the Tyee class—fish over 30 pounds—are awesome when hooked on a fly in saltwater. They often rip out 200-yards of line on the first run, and bigger fish sometimes just don't stop. I've had them charge blindly into a strangle of kelp and rush flat-out across shallows, and I've watched them just shake their head ten feet from the end of my rod then turn and swim slowly, stubbornly away. But virtually all have been wild, crashing, powerful when hooked in the open ocean. On this small river I was skeptical. I'd hooked enough salmon in moving waters to know they don't always leave their school, and the smaller the river the less chance they would. Either that or they would head back on a one-way trip for the ocean.

"Boats" for this trip were 8-foot prams and three of us started our drift by anchoring at the head of Loeb Pool. I was used to casting lead-core in the salt and quickly got into a controlled rhythm in the tight space allowed. The technique was simple: using a short leader with 8-pound-test tippet and a size 6 orange/pink yarn fly, we would cast across the current and let out line until the shooting taper bumped bottom, then while keeping "in-touch" with the bottom, more line would be given in a lift and drop technique. Many times as my line softly dragged over a fish I would instinctively strike resulting in a couple of foul-hooked fish that were quickly broken off (this typical reaction to a "take" is why fly fishers are sometimes called snaggers by locals along the Chetco).

With so many fish stratified in the pool below us no one wanted to go anywhere, so our "drift" that day turned out to be pretty short. Eventually, on one of what had become purely mechanical casts into the gently swirling dark water there was a soft tap-tap, and I slowly lifted my rod to wrenching heaviness.

We discovered something about one-man prams that day: While they are an absolute delight on the river—lightweight, easy to row and anchor even in the swiftest rapids—they are next to impossible to maneuver alone if you have to chase a big fish. We solved the problem with the buddy system. Whenever someone would hook-up, his partner would reel in and hustle over to help by lifting the fighter's anchor and putting it in the stern of the second (partner's) boat. The partner could then row both boats up or downstream and let the fighter stay tuned-in to his fish. I got very good at it since my fishing partner hooked at least fifteen fish, including one monster of 52 pounds (official) that virtually pulled both prams upstream through a strong current for 100-yards on one run!

But we hadn't yet invented the buddy system when I first hooked my fish. Things went well for the first ten minutes. The fish was content to swim in a wide circle of current and backeddy, not wanting to leave the school (just as I had suspected). It was not the rush and crash I was used to from ocean salmon, but the power was still there, 20-feet below me. I applied all the pressure I dared, and just which of us was in control became a certainty when the fish decided enough was enough. Suddenly hitting the current it turned left out of Loeb Pool and headed downstream in a line-blistering run. Jamming the rod between my knees I jerked up the anchor and rowed for all I was worth...with line still ripping out. Four hundred feet below the fish stopped in rock-strewn Willow Hole. Dropping the oars I reeled frantically as the current swept me along in slowly spinning circles.

There were four boats anchored at Willow and for a few minutes I was good entertainment hanging on to my rod with one hand and trying to row and reel with the other. Somehow I got through, floated across the hole and ended up below my fish. I dropped anchor and breathed deeply. I once heard Lefty Kreh tell a group that only two things should happen when you fight a fish, "Line should either come in or go out." So I leaned on my rod and made the fish move. It headed out of Willow Hole, back upriver towards Loeb.

Perhaps it was curiosity or the fact that he had been through it a couple of times himself that made my fishing partner follow me. Whichever, when I was sure it was all over he told me to put my anchor in the back of his boat, pull up tight, and he'd tow me. The buddy system was born.

The fish did indeed go back to its school. We beached across from the pool and I fought it from a shallow bar while twenty bait guys cheered me on. Finally, bright chrome sides, cobalt blue back with the unmistakable black spots of a Chinook, the beautiful female lay on her side gasping in six-inches of water.

Before I could react someone jumped in with a scale and hoisted the fish. "Wow, 35 pounds. That's a beauty, bud, and with a fly in the mouth, too!" Emotionally I removed the hook and in deeper water held the fish upright, gently moving it back and forth, mentally encouraging her to revive. In the shade of the canyon it was some moments before I noticed blood flowing freely from one of her gills. I looked up at my partner and he understood. He killed her quickly and efficiently.

I'll never know if my hook killed that prime fish or the guy with the scale. It doesn't matter. It died at my hand and I wasn't proud.

There's more to the story, but in short every member of our group of six killed fish on the Chetco that week. A couple, like mine, had to be. Others were because we wanted to show off our skill and achievement and because we all liked the taste of fresh salmon. Everyone said they felt bad, but truthfully we each enjoyed our "success!"

Yet, to journey so far to return to a home river, beating the odds and predators and the cruel side of nature for so long, then to get hammered in the one place they should be safe...somehow that's a tragic indignity for such an admirable creature.

So I don't cast to Chinooks in rivers anymore. Not because I don't enjoy catching them wherever I can, it's just that now I feel more strongly than ever about only doing it in saltwater. My trip back to the Chetco reinforced that. And I agree: *The same thing can happen in the ocean*. No question! But in the open sea they are wild and free to react to the hook in undisciplined madness...assuming you can find them to cast to. They aren't corralled out there! A "take" in saltwater is the real thing, not just the instinctive reaction to something they dimly remember used to be food. You must truly delude them, just like a selectively feeding trout. They are not schooled in shallow, walled corridors where cast after cast will eventually move one to react, either out of anger from the continuous bother, or because inborn forces cause it to protect itself or a mate by taking away the perceived danger to their final act. Hook one out in that immense expanse where fish have a positive advantage and you've accomplished something. Land one and you'll earn some respect!

And before anyone says it, let me state that I understand not everyone has the means or the physical ability to pursue salmon in the open ocean and that casting to them in rivers is the only way some can enjoy this sport. The comments I make about not fishing for salmon in rivers is *my* opinion, *my* philosophy, based on *my* feelings. For the record, I love the rush of water against my waders as much as anyone else, and when I play a fish in a river I know it has a better than good chance of gaining freedom even before I land it. I truly love that and I get excited just remembering past experiences! I have chosen not to fish that way any longer, but I fully realize there are many individuals who can never experience what I do on the open ocean. For them I feel sincere lament.

I also do not profess to be the best or the most knowledgeable or the smartest open ocean salmon fly fisher. But I *am* one of the first who has pursued it with total passion and commitment. For the most part I have been alone in my endeavors and as such I had to develop whatever techniques and methods have so far been successful. Early on I had to use equipment that wasn't suited to a saltwater program and patterns that didn't work, and many times I almost gave up when my efforts failed while trollers and moochers and Buzz Bombers caught fish all around me.

But gradually I was able to string together a few things that worked and as my success improved others began to take interest. Combined ideas and intense trial and error have resulted in the creation of patterns that catch fish, specialized equipment that makes the job easier—but still far from perfect— and methods and techniques that have reached a level of success I might never have arrived at on my own.

Present day equipment has undergone marvelous improvement just in the past decade, especially rods and reels, and it is no longer a fantasy to think you can catch any ocean critter that swims. I've been fortunate to have caught—or at least hooked—many saltwater species because of the efforts of guys like Lefty Kreh and Mark Sosin, Stu Apte, Billy Pate and others, who wrote about or filmed their accomplishments and gave the rest of us a successful starting point.

Open ocean salmon seem to be the only North American gamefish that still pose a mystery to fly fishers. Techniques used for sailfish and marlin, tarpon, bonefish, permit and the like are highly specialized for each species, and are well documented (and none are suitable for salmon—believe me I have tried many of them). As well, methods that take salmon are very refined, with the added intricacy that personal physical condition and environmental circumstances often limit what can be accomplished. Unless you have been out there facing the waves, winds, currents and tides it will be difficult to imagine what I'm trying to convey in the following pages. But we *are* at a place in time where what has so far been discovered about ocean salmon fishing can be discussed.

The evolution of open ocean salmon techniques is certainly on-going...we are constantly discovering and modifying. As I write this, Bob Jones and Dave Lornie are working on shorter, heavier braided heads to be used with the newly developed smaller diameter shooting lines to take flies quickly down to levels where only downriggers go. New materials may eliminate the need for full saltwater fly lines altogether and allow us to work deeper water in tidal currents and even during wind conditions that have so far stymied our efforts. They might also make distance casting easier and the use of lighter weight rods more feasible. Imagine being able to get down where fish are in 50- or 60-feet of water using a shooting taper with the equivalent sink-rate of 700- or 850-grains, but using a 9- or 10-weight rod, and having 50-pound-test backing with the same diameter as 20-pound-test monofilament. With lighter rods, 8-, 10- and 12-pound-test tippets are not subjected to the stresses that a 12-weight or heavier rod applies, and because salmon flies are often small—one to three inches—flies can be tied directly to the weight-class tippet, **not** to a shock tippet that is attached to a weight-class tippet.

I recently experimented with a 10-foot, 8/9-weight rod, a new small diameter shooting taper with Spectron line and 8-pound tippet. I landed a 23 pound Chinook quickly and with ease, but broke off another with a heavy-handed setup, and a third that got into kelp. Obviously this is not enough information to claim the new system is a success, but we're definitely on the right track. Stay tuned...

Certainly there are other fly fishers along the west coast who are just as successful at catching open ocean salmon as the small group I fish with—perhaps even more so—and in no way do I mean to detract from their position by writing about mine. It's a proven fact that most "firsts" have a parallel somewhere and that most inventions have simultaneous discoverers, sometimes thousands of miles apart, who didn't know about each other. So it is, I'm certain, with this "first" on open ocean salmon on flies. If only I knew you we could discover together...and who knows *how* far we might advance!

When I arrived in BC, so many years ago, I was fresh out of university and too puffed-up with self-assurance to hear "experts" who said it was impossible to catch salmon on cast flies in the ocean. All I knew was I could no longer pursue Chinooks in moving water so I countered arguments with reminders that fishermen—including some of them—had been trolling so-called bucktail flies and catching coho and Chinook as far back as anyone could remember. Plus, they are easily taken on flies in rivers so why not in saltwater? It made perfect sense to me.

But they smiled smug smiles that said, "You'll see, you smart young puppy..."

So began my transition.

EQUIPMENT

New techniques, methods, and specialized equipment described in the previous section notwithstanding, fly fishing equipment used for Pacific salmon is not complicated. Much of what I discuss will probably sound primitive to fly fishers who have developed equipment for and refined their techniques on more exotic saltwater species. But please bear with me...us open ocean salmon guys are still in a state of infancy.

As I mention throughout, I like a 9-foot, 8- or 9-weight rod with a strong butt and fast-tip for shallow top-water (down to 30-feet), and a 10- or sometimes 12-weight rod for deep water Chinooks, halibut and other bottomfish. Generally, a 9-weight rod will handle even the biggest salmon if the rest of your gear is top quality and there is plenty of backing on your reel. To enjoy coho, chum or pink salmon to the fullest I use a 6-weight rod...but don't go any smaller because you just might nail a big Chinook when you least expect it!

Reels *must* be the best you can afford. A fast-running Chinook can cook lesser reels. I use two for salmon: a 578 Pflueger Supreme anti reverse (which has been out of production for awhile) and a No. 4 Fin-Nor. I also have a 789 STH light saltwater cassette reel for my lighter rods, but I haven't tried it on salmon yet. Any good quality saltwater reel with a strong, dependable drag and a minimum capacity of 200-yards of 30-pound-test mono or Dacron, or equivalent diameter 50-pound-test Spectra backing, plus fly line or shooting system will work for salmon.

As you will learn from the text I also prefer shooting taper systems over full fly lines in saltwater. Not that I have anything against the long lines. Some fly fishers feel they help tire out fish more quickly dragging against more resistance, or that they can stay in better touch with their fly. Without question full lines are *much* easier to cast than shooting tapers, but I like the shooting system because heads can be changed quickly to fit conditions: floating when fish are rolling on the surface, sinking when you have to get under, and 550- to 850-grain super-fast lead-core and Deep Water Express for really deep water or fast rip-tide situations where full fly lines get carried by currents and just can't get down where they must be to be effective. Heavy rips are unusual in all but northern and inland waters around Vancouver Island, but we will talk about the very specialized techniques used to fish rips as well as deep water when there are moving currents or wind where tapers and fine diameter running lines are a necessity.

In my opinion shooting tapers offer the best versatility owing to the minimal amount of equipment you are sometimes limited to, and because they aren't as expensive to replace if a shark or other toothy creature decides to sample the finish, or if you decide to take on a prop, or if you get hung up in sharp rocks. But admittedly they are considerably more difficult to use than full lines!

If you haven't used shooting systems and want to try them, find out *how* from a qualified fly shop or an accomplished caster and then put in some practice on lawn-fish before you go fishing for real. Shooting tapers are tricky and depending on your ability and your rods they can be downright dangerous to you and anyone near you. For this reason alone, full floating, sink-tip, neutral sink, and Class IV or V sinking lines are recommended unless you plan to do a lot of open ocean fishing in future and are willing to put in the time necessary to learn to use the shooting system properly. I use both types of line and each has its own advantages.

Short *downright dangerous* story: I was after billfish off the tip of Baja in 1976. A big sailfish was attacking the bonito-meat attractor flapping in the wake of the boat and I began to false cast my shooting taper (first mistake!) as my Mexican guide stopped the panga and pulled the bait in. The sail followed it and just as I started my forward cast the fish changed direction and veered off to my left. I turned and tried to follow with my cast at the last instant (second mistake) and the 550-grain Shooting Head piled up between my shoulder blades (third mistake—you don't need to use a taper that heavy for sails. In fact a full fly line is nearly always adequate). The force knocked me to my knees and I was very fortunate not to be impaled by the hooks. When I got to shore, my wife said my back looked like I'd taken forty lashes. Felt like it, too. (P.S. It hasn't happened since!).

I presently use 100-foot Cortland .027 level running lines (shooting lines) made specifically for casting with shooting tapers. I feel they are easier to handle than monofilament or the new braided mono running lines, and the casting distances or sink rates sacrificed in normal saltwater conditions are not worth measuring. In fast moving currents and deep water it's a different story, but nothing that can't be overcome. If you decide to use a straight mono running line, go with Sunset's red Amnesia or Hal Janssen's clear Leader Control, available in 200-foot spools, in 25-pound-test. Both straighten easily and when used with a stripping basket (I prefer a plastic baby bathtub Velcroed to the floor of my boat) neither pose any unusual tangle problems. Watch setups and fast runs, though. Any running line will cut to the bone if handled improperly or grabbed at the wrong time. I've got the scars to prove it!

Leaders for saltwater fly fishing are important, but not *as* important as they are, say, when trout fishing on a spring creek. I use a couple of feet of stiff 30-pound for the butt section (I'm also trying new braided loop connectors, and so far I really like them) and a standard 9-foot leader tapered to .015 or .017. Then about three feet of 8-, 10- or 12-pound straight monofilament as a tippet for smaller salmon species, and for deep-water Chinook 20-pound-test isn't too heavy. Fairly stiff leaders turn over large saltwater flies better than limp stuff, and using a loop knot to connect the fly allows good fly movement in the water. I used to tie my own tapered leaders, but I found in saltwater there is just too much debris that catches on the knots. Seven or so feet of straight 20-pound-test tied directly to the butt section, plus a tippet works well also (or a 3/4 to 1/4 ratio). Lefty Kreh wrote about this combination in his book *Fly Fishing in Salt Water* saying it was as good as a tapered leader. I resort to it often when I don't have a tapered leader and it works fine.

Leader length can also be significant. Short leaders are all right for coho, pink, chum and sockeye salmon, but while Chinooks are not known to be leader-shy, they *can* be extremely finicky so try to use at least a seven- to nine-foot leader with three- or four-feet of weight-class tippet (no shock tippet) with a loop knot connecting the fly. If things don't look right or the fly doesn't act properly, Chinook just won't hit. I've watched dozens over the years follow or charge a fly, then veer off because something wasn't true. Often it was the fly pattern or my retrieve, but just as often I feel it was the leader and how it was making the fly act. Oh, and one other thing—change leaders often. I sometimes use two or three in a long day of fishing. Depending on the area you are apt to catch far more "other" fish than salmon and they will drag you into the rocks, through kelp, over sand...even their own scales can be abrasive when they roll on the line. Check tippets and leaders often and change or cut off a section whenever there is a nick or abrasion or unusual kinking. I promise it will eventually cost you a salmon if you don't!

FLY PATTERNS

Throughout the book I mention personal patterns, like Firecrackers, Improved Polar Herring, Polar Shrimp, squid, and a few patterns I have purchased. The flies to use depend on the species of salmon you are after and the baitfish present in the area. Somewhere in the book are photographs of patterns, but as stated elsewhere almost any fly will work if it represents food, and if you hunt long enough and put yourself into feeding fish. Just be sure your fly reasonably matches size and color of bait and then concentrate on your retrieve which I feel is the most important aspect (described as we go along). And in case I forget to mention it, I try not to use stainless-steel hooks. Breakoffs are fairly common as is cutting the leader when a hook is deep. Stainless doesn't dissolve in a fish's maw or stomach. Better to waste a few flies from saltwater corrosion and have to throw them out than decree a slow, agonizing death.

Patterns should match two-inch to four-inch herring, needlefish (sand lance) and anchovy in top water; larger if you fish deep. For sockeye, very small size 10 (maybe half an inch to one inch) sparse red, olive green, or fluorescent pink shrimp flies, or Hootchies split into three sections (tie on one section that has two or three strands and pinch off some of the tentacle length). You only need to match color with these.

In general, take two rods, two reels, an extra running line, extra backing, and two each floating and sinking shooting tapers—or full fly lines on spools—and lots of leader and tippet material (IGFA tippet material if you're after records), and fly patterns. And take along a small tying kit if you are a fly tier. None of this stuff is available in the country we're going to be fishing.

This and the information that follows will get you started. As you progress in knowledge and ability you will surely innovate new methods, techniques and even modify equipment and fly patterns. As mentioned, the group I fish with is always modifying and changing, and we are right now on the verge of some really neat advances touched on earlier. I sincerely hope these and other breakthroughs can be written about and published in various fly fishing magazines as they occur...perhaps I'll even have an opportunity to update and revise this book in a few years. But for now we have to go with our limited knowledge about this exciting new frontier.

ONE

THE INCREDIBLE SALMONIDS

*T*his first chapter is a little tedious, but any discussion about salmon must give some background, known history and ocean-going habits of catchable species, and future potential. I consulted with people at several levels of the Canadian Department of Fisheries and Oceans (DFO), provincial fisheries biologists from British Columbia, state biologists from Washington and Oregon, read stacks of published U.S. and Canadian government materials, had discussions with knowledgeable peers and a professional biologist from Seattle, and relied on articles and my own experience to develop this information. I believe it's as reliable and accurate as my often-biased mind allows.

THE BIG PICTURE

(From CAT #EN21-117/1-1992, Environment Canada & Fisheries and Oceans)

Canada has a Green Plan, a national challenge to preserve their environment. I'm sure the U.S. has one as well, but I haven't seen it defined like this:

> "Respect for nature requires us to accept our responsibility as its stewards. We do not own the environment. It is a trust we must protect for the benefit of current and future generations. The same ingenuity and innovative spirit that we have devoted to improving our standard of living must now be used to help preserve the quality of the environment."
>
> *Govt. of Canada, 1990*

Sounds good. Words spoken in the heat of emotion to pacify the masses often do. Bureaucratic smoke. Sort of like "good guys" riding in to save the town after it's been ravaged. I sure want to believe it, but I fear the usual disappointment with all such grand government designs will be the real result. Still, let's look at it (but be warned, while the outline I present does have potential, so far nothing tangible has been accomplished so my dialog reflects my disheartenment. Perhaps you will be able to form a more positive opinion).

The Green Plan initiatives for British Columbia will effect the entire west coast: One, labeled the "Fraser River Action Plan," is a six-year federal program introduced in 1991 by Environment Canada and Fisheries and Oceans Canada to improve the overall health of the Fraser River ecosystem as a means of ensuring survival of existing salmon populations and to rebuild salmon stocks to historic levels. A gigantic project! The Fraser River is heralded as the greatest salmon producing river system in the world. It drains nearly one quarter of the entire province—more than 145,000 square miles—an area the size of Great Britain. It has been home to First Nations people for more than 10,000 years, and today more than two million people from every layer of life inhabit its expanse. And it's a mess.

The population within this drainage basin has doubled in 30 years, and is expected to double again in the next 20. Dams, water diversions and draw downs, poor water quality, industry, agriculture and urbanization have caused significant losses of fish and wildlife habitat all along its banks.

Timber cut has increased four-fold within the basin, and pulp and paper mills are discharging dioxins, furans and other toxins into the river system to go along with the pesticides and herbicides from agriculture and forestry activities, and chemicals from mining.

Greater Vancouver, one of the most beautiful coastal city-aggregations anywhere, discharges sewage treated only to the lowest required levels directly into the Fraser estuary, and atmospheric pollution is causing problems throughout the lower Fraser Valley and creeping into northern Washington state.

Obviously this Green Plan isn't designed just to save salmonids in the Fraser River. With over 60 municipalities, 96 native Indian bands, and hundreds of individual settlements established along its 820-mile length, the ultimate goal is to create a healthier economic-social environment as well, and the federal action plan list designed to accomplish this is long. Still, salmonids are the major heritage from British Columbia rivers and natives in particular look on their stewardship as a sacred trust.

In 1984 Ron Sparrow, a native Musqueam Indian, was charged with food fishing using an illegal net at the mouth of the Fraser River. His tribe challenged the law that prohibited this. Six years later the Supreme Court of Canada ruled that aboriginal communities, under the Constitution of Canada, have first rights to fish "...for food, social and ceremonial purposes." As a result of the Sparrow Decision native Indians acquired constitutional assurance that they have claim to the resource over all other users, and further, they must be consulted before additional allocations are allowed to any other group!

The majority of outside users do not like the ruling (does the Boldt Decision ring a bell here?) for obvious reasons, but with the ruling backing them, British Columbia native Indians are now developing their own green plan which will no doubt be either the most effective, or the most destructive, of all the plans.

Because the anadromous fishery has been the cornerstone for so many generations of native communities their ambition is to preserve and rebuild their societies and economies around it. To help implement their plan, the Canadian government is spending $140 million nationally over the next seven years...mostly for on-the-job training of native Indians in fishery-management. The expectation is native administration will result in a more stable, predictable and profitable fishery for all user groups. If tribal cultural instincts to preserve-what-nature-provides-and-use-only-what-is-necessary are applied, then it has the potential to be a successful program. On the other hand if radical native factions prevail, it will be disastrous.

In 1992, to make implementation of the plans easier and to reduce opportunity for misunderstanding and conflict between various individual native cultures over fishing rights, the Pearse Report recommended one agreement be negotiated with all tribal units living on each major British Columbia river system rather than separate agreements with each individual band or tribe. In 1993 such an agreement was reached with Skeena River tribal groups in northern BC, and many bands along the Fraser reached an historic accord of cooperation among themselves based on traditional shares and requirements. Not the whole package, but a beginning.

Every user group—commercial, recreational and native—needs assurance the fishery will remain stable and viable. A tough challenge given the Sparrow Decision conferred complete title to tribal authority. But there is one safeguard: the decision did allow for as yet unquantified conservation needs to be met before any "rights" to the fishery resource can be utilized. It did not decree a specific allotment of fish (compared to the Boldt Decision that gave 50 percent of the fish to natives) but rather left fisheries management to the specialists. There is little doubt, however, that if equitable sharing of the resource is not realized the court will impose a settlement.

There is also significant environmental clout associated with BC natives' rights to anadromous fish that has not yet been realized. One question that needs to be answered is whether or not their right to fish implies assurances that fish will always be available. If this is the case then water use or abuse on spawning river systems will require close scrutinization for any negative impacts on fish stocks, and if there are then forestry, mining, farming, industry, fishing, power company and domestic users will be required to clean-up their methods.

I'm explaining this not because I enjoy techni-stuff, but because if there is any positive potential in our future, this is it. The Sparrow Decision requires a fundamental change in the way fisheries are to be managed in Canada. It challenges every user level to cooperate closely in sustaining and harvesting the resource, and while the relationship is still fragile, it is a decisive step towards improvement.

Habitat loss, all over the west, has been and continues to be a major problem with our fisheries, and the forest industry receives the largest share of bad press. That attitude won't change in what I write here, but the plain fact is, in the overall scheme of things what the foresters do is temporary. Certainly there is a negative impact on the immediate future—and in some cases, permanent damage is caused—but nature is very forgiving and the effects of today will be gone in 40 or 50 years. Unfortunately the remaining stocks of fish don't have that long and various state and provincial governments and the forest industry seem to finally be recognizing this.

A joint government/industry program is underway in British Columbia aimed at better forest management for the protection of fish. Patterned after a successful environmental rehab program in Oregon, the BC program will use displaced forest workers to clean and rehabilitate streams, replant brush and trees along banks, plant and stabilize slide areas, and close logging roads. It's a very big first step and if it continues it will solidify the sincere intentions of both groups to work together towards something other than their own bottom lines. You will read accounts of forest degradation in the following pages about which I am very opinionated and emotional. But the latest news—while still tentative—is positive. Keep your fingers crossed!

Yet with all this being said, the most damaging long-term impact on fish habitat simply is us! Growth continues and subdivisions blossom everywhere...and that's not going to change! The result is a continual lowering of an already precarious water table with used water being returned to the environment as enriched effluent from houses built right next to streams and lakes (I myself live within a short cast of a very fishy 50 acre private lake that is slowly dying from phosphate intrusion and water reduction). Trailer parks (or modular home parks—whatever the politically correct term is now), golf courses, shopping malls, schools, warehouses, etc., all add to the problem as vital estuaries and marshes are filled and blacktopped and streams are diverted or channelized. It goes on and on.

Green Plans and rehabilitation programs hold great possibilities for both U.S. and Canadian fishery stocks and for the environment in general, but while there has been marvelous planning and mountains of paper pushing, there has been very little action and no real change in the historic performance of failing to protect the fragile remaining habitat. Unless there is action with a capital A soon, I'm afraid government's propensity to mendacity will once again be revealed. "Tell them what they want to hear, promise them anything...it'll die down as soon as something else comes along to divert their attention."

A Washington state biologist puts it in perspective: "I would rather see a clear-cut than a K Mart," and while neither is acceptable it comes down to the lesser of two evils. Say what you will about the Sparrow Decision but it may be the only saving influence in the future of our west coast fisheries, assuming the natives act on it in a responsible manner. It sure as hell isn't going to happen with the bureaucrats.

SALMON ENHANCEMENT

We might not even have it as good as we do on the west coast if not for yet another plan in place since 1977 in British Columbia. The Federal-Provincial Salmonid Enhancement Program—SEP—came into being to "correct past mistakes" and has become an extremely significant factor in the present recreational and commercial west coast salmon fishery.

By the 1970s everyone from California to Alaska knew there was a serious problem with our salmon. What was once considered such a vast resource that it couldn't possibly be depleted had declined to a state that angered every user. In the words of Canada's DFO officials, "There was little understanding of the overall environmental needs of anadromous fish. Consequently, rivers were polluted, dams were constructed and spawning beds were destroyed, not to mention excessive commercial over-harvest. Over time, fishermen noticed there were fewer and fewer fish." No kidding! A brief history tells all:

An Excerpt from: *This Is SEP*
(Canadian Department of Fisheries and Oceans publication)

The sheer volume of fish in these waters in the early days was overwhelming. Almost every stream and river hosted a run of one or more of the five species of salmon and the two species of sea-run trout that are classified as "salmonids."

The first salmon were exported, salted, from Fort Langley (BC) in the mid-1800's. In only a few short years the method for commercial canning of fish was developed and the industry boomed. Canneries lined the BC coast. At first, they were very wasteful. They took only the most prized fish for canning, the sockeye, and dumped other species their nets gathered. It was not uncommon for thousands of dead fish to line the riverbanks near the canneries.

Other economic activities were also having an impact on the resource. Logging methods often scoured spawning beds to bedrock or smothered them with silt. Road building activities tore up the gravels or created impassable barriers. Pollutants, especially in an era when little was known about chemical buildup, began to accumulate in salmon streams.

Over the first 70 years of the 20th century the sizes of salmon catches decreased steadily and alarmingly. At first, only the fishing industry really cared, but gradually everyone began to see that the declines were affecting them. The lost economic opportunities were costing jobs, especially in small coastal communities where fishing had been a major source of income.

A joint industry-government seminar in BC in the mid-1970's called for solutions. Hearings were held around the province to seek public opinion. Agreement came from every side: A program to reverse the trend and restore the stocks was essential and was finally implemented in 1977.

The main goal of the Salmonid Enhancement Program was to double the population of salmonids produced in BC waters, restoring stocks to pre-1900 levels by the early 1990s (an interesting concept since no formal inventories of pre-1900 fish populations were ever taken or accurately reported, other than "There were lots of fish..."). The federal DFO took on responsibility for management and enhancement of the five salmon species, and the British Columbia provincial Fisheries Branch became responsible for steelhead and cutthroat trout. The public also desired direct involvement and—remarkably, I think, for a government organization—SEP responded positively and all factions were able to closely interact.

SEP was committed to rebuilding all stocks so a number of enhancement techniques were tested and modified, and eventually the most beneficial were adopted as the program progressed. Hatchery incubation and spawning, and outdoor rearing tanks and ponds came first. Then semi-natural enhancement methods gained favor: fish ladders around blockages and dams; spawning channels to extend natural spawning areas; and in-stream incubation boxes. And finally direct enhancement to natural spawning areas through habitat restoration, enrichment of nursery lakes and marshes through fertilization to increase growth of basic food chain components, and control of pollutants. Naturally certain salmon species became more important over time as cost-benefit ratios were evaluated among user groups.

Results have been eyebrow-raising to say the least: Compared to only ten percent survival in nature, in hatchery environments Chinook and coho have shown an egg-to-fry survival of just under 90 percent, while chum and pink salmon have produced over 90 percent according to DFO-printed statistics. Sockeye spawning is not so successful in hatcheries but does show up to 50 percent egg survival in outdoor spawning channels, and enrichment of lake nursery environments increases survival of wild sockeye fry dramatically.

Work to enhance habitat conditions along many streams and rivers to help wild spawning of all species also continues. School children, natives, and other community groups have taken up the cause all along the coast and inland along spawning streams. Even city dwellers help by painting street drains with fish characterizations to remind people not to dump pollutants. Aside from the obvious comparison to wild-born survival-of-the-fittest, SEP-produced fish are having a positive impact on every user group. Hundreds of millions of dollars spent for a single purpose and public acceptance of the concept does that!

Without question there have been benefits to salmonid stocks. Nearly half of sports-caught coho in British Columbia over the past ten years were reportedly SEP fish. By 1994, although certain runs remained in danger, some were rebuilding, and a few sockeye stocks were approaching historic levels. From all appearances the success of these efforts—whatever else is said about the agencies involved—has been favorable. But perhaps euphoria paints a better portrait.

SEP was launched to reverse a trend—the serious decline of a major resource and a vital part of human heritage. As I write this, curtailed funding of the SEP is into its second year because of the old "severe budget restraints" syndrome. But listen to this: The BC Wildlife Federation is reporting that there are approximately 60 senior bureaucrats (read pedantic officials) in the Department of Fisheries and Oceans in Ottawa who draw over $6 million a year in salaries *plus* perks, office costs, travel, salaries of personal staff, etc. Does government cut some of this officious staff or their salaries or overhead? Heck no...they cut money for eco-studies, SEP funding and enforcement instead. Smoke and bureaucrats!

The salmon fishery along the Washington-Oregon-California coastline has just taken another nose dive. Seasons for coho and Chinook salmon have been heavily curtailed and even closed. I honestly don't know if there is a correlation to the reduced SEP spending but some runs of juvenile coho and Chinook migrate south after leaving brood waters in BC. That's not to say the Oregon-Washington fishery is dependent on British Columbia fish, but apparently the same scenario might occur in Canada in the future. In May 1994 I phoned an administrator with SEP in Vancouver, BC to ask about the projected effects of spending cuts and was told, "We might be looking at closing part of the salmon fishery along inland BC waters as well, and will take it one season at a time into the future."

Apparently there is concern that with the U.S. west coast fishery closed and stocks suffering a severe downturn, excessive pressure from U.S. fishermen might further damage BC stocks. I *can* say that there was definitely an increase in American traffic—especially from Washington state—during an August '94 trip I made to Tofino, but whether or not that translates into a problem is up to the bureaucrats. The BC resort owners and local fishermen I talked with sure don't have a problem with it.

I was also told that it isn't immediately obvious whether reduced SEP spending will actually cause an offsetting reduction in salmon stocks, but the fact *they* question it leads me to conclude that is how they view the situation. Personally, I feel there are factors at work influencing the fishery that are *far* bigger than even the government... We'll get to those in a moment.

First, time for a quick tantrum: As I often proclaim—from my best wide-eyed post-yuppie state of mind—I have great faith that the future of fisheries is going to be all right. But critics always pop my bubble by reminding me it is all artificial. The monies from SEP and Canada's Green Plan and funding of the native Indians' own plan for saving their salmon heritage...all this ongoing work will implode when the money stops because the cure is still being ignored (*if* it is really even known!). Until the issues of dams, perverse logging methods, mining and industrial and domestic pollution, over-harvesting by commercial *and* recreational fishermen, and decimation of the salmonid food supply are all corrected at the source, nothing will be solved. Bad things will just continue to continue. Where is the remedy in pouring millions upon millions of dollars into environmental and fish-producing programs that must continually be funded or the entire structure will collapse? Thousands of government and civilian appointments have been created with such programs, and timber, mining and fishing jobs are being preserved—for now. But eventually that edifice will come shattering down.

I realize these comments will offend certain people. I have no quarrel with the hard-working individuals who earn their livings directly or indirectly from natural resources. They do what governments allow, and that's fair...it's how our system works. But there should be space for every user group to work and play and benefit.

And I don't mean to sound like a government-basher either. Monies spent on social and economic programs are a fact of life, and if some spills over onto natural resources, hey, who am I to question it? But wake up! None of you will have jobs in your chosen industries if the root problems aren't corrected. For now I choose to believe there still is a future to look forward to, despite bureaucrats who continue to believe their own bureaucratese. But for how long? OK, I'm done now.

ANOTHER PIECE OF THE MYSTERY

You might want to be sitting down for this. For all I have stated about green plans, SEP, bureaucrats, and other bad guys ad-nausea, out on the high seas a new study by state and provincial biologists might have uncovered what could be the real cause of the decline of salmon along the west coast. Ancient scale samples of anchovy, herring, other baitfishes and salmon taken from different layers of sediments along the Continental Shelf indicate the present downturn in salmon stocks that we are experiencing might well be a natural cycle that has occurred in the past.

Nutrients produced near the ocean surface, or in deep water and brought to the surface by upsurging currents, provide feed for the lower end of the salmon food chain...and for young salmon themselves when they first enter the sea. If these nutrients are not present all species that depend on them directly, and their predators, must either travel vast distances in search of feed...or perish.

Climatic changes—such as El Niño—can cause water temperature shifts that in only a few years dramatically effect the production of the feed plank-tons. When such changes occur in conjunction with a man-made impact like over-harvesting a species (anchovies along the California and Oregon coasts for example, or herring in British Columbia) the results can be disastrous.

Right now we are faced with a major depreciation factor in our California-Oregon-Washington-British Columbia salmon fishery—especially with coho salmon—and none of the government organizations or scientists are willing to say the cause is due positively to natural phenomena, which is in truth a valid viewpoint given what is known. It's much more uncomplicated to blame all the known enemies like the logging and mining industries, dams, domestic and industrial pollution, reduction of SEP funding, etc., like I do, but unofficial con-jecture is that while these certainly contribute to the reduction, atmospheric and climatic changes in the late 70s and early 80s modified Pacific waters and creat-ed the present significant decline in our fishery here. And according to a January 1995 *USA Today* report, El Ninõ has returned to the west coast! Warmer waters in the southern Pacific and higher temperatures in the northern Pacific waters are being blamed for the 1994-95 torrential rains and heavy snows in California and unseasonably high winter temperatures across much of the nation. It is not certain what this will do to our fishing, but recent history gives us some strong indications. It's the old "God works in mysterious ways..." thing, and if *that's* not bigger than government and everything else, I don't know what is.

The other side of the mystery is that whenever such a disaster transpires in one area, an offsetting balance seems to occur somewhere else. Northern British Columbia and Alaska are experiencing just the opposite conditions. Salmon production there is absolutely booming and while no one can say exactly why, the reasons seem evident since their increased productivity coincides almost exactly with the decline here. That, combined with evidence that salmon spawned in British Columbia and Oregon are being caught in Alaskan waters in higher quantities than ever before, tells me we should be paying at least as much attention to natural phenomenon factors as those induced by man. For sure there isn't much that can be done about the big "G" factor, and the bad guys sure aren't off the hook here, but this possibility should be considered to say the least!

LIFE CYCLES

(From various Canadian Department of Fisheries and Oceans pamphlets, periodicals, and other publications).

The following information is based on known and validated historical spawning and movement habits of salmonids and does not take into account the recent influences on Pacific coast waters by changing climatic conditions mentioned in the previous section. The official scientific jury is still out on those effects...although I do reserve the right to interject certain strong personal conclusions periodically.

At some period each year British Columbia waters host all five Pacific coast salmon during their migration cycles, plus steelhead and sea-run cutthroat. The length of time spent at sea varies by species—and even within a given species. Some Canadian-born salmon spend as many as seven years in the ocean, ranging as far south as San Francisco Bay in California and north into the Arctic Ocean, before returning to their own stream of origin to spawn. Conversely, Sacramento, Smith, Chetco and Columbia River salmon are known to swim through BC waters in their migration circuits, as do salmon from Alaska. Sometimes all these schools intermingle and create immense populations during certain summer months along the outer coast of Vancouver Island and all around the Queen Charlottes. So much volume—even now—within easy reach of fly fishers is the primary reason I chose to write about BC waters.

Each run or stock is totally unique in genetic make-up and adapted specifically to its own home waters. Colder northern streams, for example, might be lethal on eggs from southern sockeye stocks, and some Chinook runs would have difficulty spawning in small streams. That's why it is so important to control logging and pollution on all spawning streams and rivers: Entire genetic strains can be wiped out in one careless season of man-made disasters.

I won't go into the egg/milt thing here...I'm sure everyone knows how that works, but suffice to say it takes literally thousands of years for evolution to create the proper genetic program for a specific run to navigate a specific migration route over thousands of miles which ends back in one specific stream. If spawning habitat has been eliminated, so will be that unique run. Other than for perhaps a few individual fish by virtue of a marvelous accident, the greater part of the run doesn't have the *choice* to simply move over to some other stream. They aren't programmed for it! Fish or fertile eggs or fry can be transplanted to other waters by man in an attempt to create or restock a run...but according to the experts it just doesn't normally happen on its own.

SALMON DISTRIBUTION

Coho: Native peoples along the Pacific slope of North America depended on these salmon for thousands of years, and recreational fishermen today rely on coho—silvers—as the mainstay of saltwater sport fishing. Historically they have been the most dependable of all species, remaining relatively close to home waters throughout their short three-year life span (up to five-years in some far northern and Alaskan waters) and usually staying near or less than 100 miles from coastal shores, although recent studies have shown some schools to be far beyond the 200-mile limit apparently in search of feed as it declines along the coast.

Hatched in streams from California to Alaska, coho spend their first year—and sometimes two—in freshwater, then move into the salt as smolts. Their freshwater needs are different from all other salmon in that they require a cleaner environment and more feed which allows them to enter the hostile ocean environment somewhat larger. Having a naturally aggressive behavior, survival is high if they have a good nursery. They are even *built* aggressively with an oversized tail and an in-your-face attitude that keeps them in continuous motion and *always* on the feed, which is why I believe they are the easiest of all salmon to catch. Find a bait school and coho will nearly always be close by. That's important for fly fishers to know. Patterns that match feed size and color, and retrieves that imitate wounded images will consistently take fish!

Consider that coho from our southern coastal waters spawn as three-year-olds, and in that short time individuals in some runs reached 30 pounds. Until the mid-70s it was not uncommon to catch so-called "northern" coho over 20 pounds in the fall...but that is rare along our southern coast now (more on northern coho in the Campbell River section). The gene pool that created those magnificent specimens disappeared long ago, except in northern BC and Alaskan waters where they are said to be stable. Adults caught down here are more commonly four to 12 pounds, still an amazing growth achievement given the conditions they face and the degradation of traditional forage from commercial anchovy and herring over-fishing, and natural environmental factors that we may only now be uncovering.

Another quick tantrum: It blows my mind that the Canadian DFO allows 40,000 to 50,000 tons of herring to be squashed each spring just so aristocrats in Japan can have fish eggs on their crackers...and what isn't used for that is turned into fertilizer or cat food. Regardless of the cause, wasn't anything learned from the collapse of the anchovy fishery? If there's no feed guess what happens to salmon?

Sadly, according to the BC Recreational Fisheries Advisory Council the coho fishery in British Columbia is on the verge of collapse. Coho were very high on the SEP priority list, which means with present budget cuts the numbers previously produced under hatchery conditions will decline sharply. That, combined with the already extreme reduction of freshwater spawning and nursery habitat and feed, and feeding patterns that are keeping them in Alaskan waters for longer periods, means wild stocks will also continue to decline resulting in a disappearing fishery.

Chinook: I get drooly when I talk about Chinooks. There isn't a more exciting fish anywhere, I guess because they are *so* difficult on flies in the ocean and because weather and water conditions are often mean where they are. They have my utmost respect...a term I associate with Howie Long, 9.9 earthquakes, tornadoes and other such phenomena that can beat me to a pulp.

Like coho, Chinook also spawn in rivers from California to Alaska, with the highest production coming from large major river systems. Chinook young remain in freshwater from a few months to more than two years, but once in the ocean they migrate vast distances. Their relatively sparse numbers limit large-scale tagging studies, so ocean-going habits are not well known.

The age of Chinooks returning to spawn varies from two-year-olds to seven. Obviously the longer a fish remains in the sea foraging and feeding, the larger growth potential it has. Really big Chinooks—the 100-plus pounders—are long gone. There are still a fair number of five- and six-year old fish in northern waters around the Queen Charlotte Islands to the Gulf of Alaska that might hit 80 pounds or so, but they are few and damned far between.

Del Canty told me the story about his fly rod world record ninety-some-thing pound Chinook, or whatever it weighed, caught in an Alaskan river. Scale samples showed it to be a seven-year-old. Didn't sound any more excit-ing than my own personal-best 63 pounder from the Kitsumkalum River in BC that was so lethargic and black and scabby-ugly it was difficult to even touch it, and I sure as heck wasn't going to take a scale from it. I couldn't wait to weigh it (in the net) and give it back to the river. Given my self-righteous propensity for staying away from spawning salmon—and ridiculing those who continue to harass them—that's one tale I'm not proud of and don't intend to relate. I only mention it here for those who know of this exemplary achievement. Right!

Three-, four-, and five-year-old spawning Chinook are now common in southern coastal rivers, and in the past few years, probably because of the SEP, smaller clone-type fish now ranging in the 20 to 30 pound class seem to be the rule according to my recent experience and findings of friends who fish frequently all along the coast for Chinooks. Many rivers also have more than one run of Chinooks, some arriving in spring, some in fall, and still oth-ers later in winter, which staggers migration and spawning cycles and allows some runs to survive if a disaster occurs.

Although certain specific stocks are in serious trouble and SEP spending reductions will have a downside impact, overall, Chinook are doing much bet-ter than coho owing mostly to the fact that their freshwater needs are far differ-ent and because good numbers of wild stocks still spawn in the interior sys-tems where there has been less negative man-caused environmental impact.

I've spent some exciting times chasing these largest of salmonids. Size has rarely been the criterion because truly, deceiving one of any size is reward enough. They are tough! Many Chinook accounts will be related as we go along.

Pink Salmon: Fondly called "humpies" (for the pronounced hump on the backs of spawning males) these most prolific of all salmon species are found from California to the Bering Sea. Get into a school of these *any-where* and you'll wear yourself out. A large one will go six or seven pounds, but an average in the ocean is closer to three or four. I've caught pinks almost everywhere along the coast—casting from shore to twenty-five miles out in the ocean—and even in Lake Superior. They'll hit just about any-thing, they don't fight all that well, their mouths are exceptionally soft, and they are mushy when cooked after being frozen. Other than that they are great confidence builders! "Sea-rats" my friend George calls them. But I don't care. Go seven consecutive days without touching another salmon at

$500.00 or more a day at some exclusive fishing lodge, and see how much fun they can be!

One notable characteristic of this species is its rigidly genetic two-year life span. That's why every other year certain rivers have heavy runs of pinks that vastly outnumber the previous year's runs. There is no overlapping and spawning generally occurs in small rivers and streams that empty directly into the ocean or are near the coast. Wonderful training-bra fish.

Chum Salmon: Not much is known about this species once they enter the ocean. I've only caught a couple, and that was by accident. I was casting over about a half-acre of tiny herring right on the surface one August evening near Alert Bay on northern Vancouver Island and hooked a screamer I assumed was a coho. It did everything a coho is supposed to do for about five minutes—jumped, ran, burned my fingers, twisted, ripped the water. I had orders to keep a couple of fish for our camp group, but as I led it towards the net it resisted me like a little pit-bull terrier. Finally I threw the net around it. Ten minutes later the same tough-guy scene repeated itself with another and I headed my boat for shore with dinner.

At the cleaning table I noticed the fish for the first time. Bright blue-green head and very faint vertical bars behind bright silver sides. I didn't think much about it until I opened up the first one and saw the meat was pale orange-pink. It was only then I realized they were chums. "Are they legal?" Someone said they were, except when caught in rivers. They weren't bad eating. Mild taste and not quite as oily as Chinook tend to be. Apparently Indians preferred them for smoking and drying over other salmon for that reason.

Chum salmon reproduce in moderate size streams in Oregon, Washington, British Columbia, and as far north as the Mackenzie River in Alaska. They also range from Japan, Korea, Russia and Siberia to the Lena River in the Arctic on the Asian side of the Pacific. Fry emerge from gravel redds and move directly towards the sea where they disperse far offshore. As mentioned little is known about their migration patterns, though tagging studies have shown fish born in British Columbia waters to be in the Gulf of Alaska within a year.

And that, as they say, is that concerning my knowledge of chums! Other than in Queen Charlotte Island waters where large schools do linger, I can't say they can be targeted by fly fishers because they seem to move through other areas quickly on their way to home waters as adults. They are great, tough fighters and chances are I have caught more then the two mentioned here, but don't press me for details.

Sockeye Salmon: Of all the salmon that inhabit coastal waters, sockeye are unquestionably the most difficult to catch on a cast fly in open ocean! My affair with them began, naturally enough, on a BC river 300 miles from saltwater. Sockeye are programmed to spawn in streams that flow into lakes so their young will have one, two, or in some regions, three years in a freshwater "nursery" before their seaward migration. These fall-spawners attract resident trout that move out of lakes to gorge on loose eggs. I was after the big trout from Salmon Lake that prowled among the famous Adams River sockeye run in the south-central BC interior.

Armed with a small single-egg fly pattern and great optimism I covered about a quarter-mile of river before I realized my chances of hitting a trout among the thousands of salmon was not good. On nearly every retrieve I either foul-hooked or scratched a bright red sockeye, and even hooked the odd one in the mouth, my fly no doubt swept there by the current. Five to eight pound sockeye are marvelous fighters, especially on light trout gear in swift water, so it was with some reluctance I finally gave up my quest for trout. Harassing spawning salmon is illegal in BC and it was only going to be a matter of time before I'd be cited by one of the Fisheries personnel on the river if I didn't quit. I promised myself to come back in April or May to fish the lakes at stream mouths where those same monster trout were supposed to lie in wait for the millions of salmon fry as they made their way into nursery waters. That was in 1974 and I still haven't made it back. But I didn't forget my sockeye encounter and years later I would learn how to take them in saltwater.

Once in the ocean, sockeye parallel the coast in a northward migration. Early in life they feed primarily on zooplanktons and crustacean larvae—krill—but lacking sufficient quantities of these preferred foods they are said to turn to alternate feed such as tiny herring, needlefish fry, and seed shrimp. Their maturing years find them in a huge area of the Pacific that extends fan-like 2600 miles west out into the ocean, north as far as the Gulf of Alaska, and south to the Oregon-California border. They return as prime six to eight pound adults after two or three years at sea.

In the final weeks before heading up home river systems, adult sockeye have been known to gorge on any available feed—even herring, needlefish and shrimp—to supplement needed protein. And grabbing a baitfish is no small feat for a sockeye. They have no teeth until they reach spawning color...then teeth on the males are formidable! This piece of information on feeding habits is important to anyone contemplating sockeye in saltwater. When I finally had the opportunity to cast to them in the open ocean, I modified some of my coho flies and invented a couple of shrimp patterns. I'll relate my experiences when we get to northern Vancouver Island.

Steelhead and Cutthroat: Considered recreational and native food species, and are managed by Provincial Fisheries agents. I love steelhead and have caught my share in rivers over the years—even taken the odd one in saltwater—but wild steelhead are just about gone. My prejudice for not fishing spawners in rivers used to go right out the window when I saw a steelhead. Now I contain myself. Double-standards don't wear well with my critics.

Steelhead migration routes take them from the central California coast to the Alaska Peninsula, with major spawning centered from northern Oregon to northern British Columbia. They are said to resemble Atlantic salmon genetically and in fighting ability, which was also my conclusion after catching grilse in the Mirimichi River in New Brunswick a few years ago.

Steelhead move to the ocean as two- or three-year-old-fish and prior to spawning spend up to three more years in saltwater. A few achieve enormous sizes—in the 40 pound range—and unlike Pacific salmon which die, steelhead return to the ocean after spawning. Steelhead don't grow much after that, but they do recuperate and somewhere between 30 and 60 percent return to spawn a second time. Not much is known about their ocean habits or life expectancy once they return to saltwater.

There is an intriguing series of stories about giant trout (albeit incomplete in details) I heard while living in BC. A rainbow trout over 50 pounds was reportedly taken from Jewel Lake in southern interior BC in 1932. It was never officially weighed, so it couldn't be recognized as a world record. A year later another rainbow about the same size was caught, but it also was not properly weighed or recorded. Then, in the 1940s yet another 50+ pounder was taken from Jewel and this one *was* authenticated. However, because of "irregularities" surrounding circumstances of the catch, it could not be entered as a *Field & Stream* world record either.

I was peeing my pants to get to that lake. Believe me, it's no big deal! Pretty setting and tons of feed, but the trout are less than average size for BC lakes now. So why the monsters back then?

Tracing the stream on a map from its origin at the lake, its waters eventually connect with the Columbia River. My unprofessional guess is those big fish could have been steelhead either trapped there by nature or they just remained in Jewel Lake rather than going back to sea after spawning. The particular genetic program that led them as part of a run to a stream there would now be long-extinct.

They might also have been Gerrards, the rare strain of rainbows from Kootenay Lake that spawn in the Lardeau River. Before World War II, Gerrard strains were transplanted into many small lakes in the region as a means of "protecting" wild stock. Until then all the eggs—so to speak—were all in one place. Jewel Lake might have been one such repository.

The Kootenay River system also flows into the Columbia, and BC rainbow trout, including Gerrards, are said to be genetically akin to steelhead. And since I don't know where I'm going with this let's get back on track.

One last note on steelhead... We all know how desperate the situation is with wild steelhead, especially on once extremely prolific Skeena, Dean and Fraser River systems. In British Columbia, sport, native and commercial fishing sectors are working closely with BC Fish and Wildlife (now part of the BC Ministry of Land, Environment and Parks) and the DFO to reduce incidental commercial harvest of steelhead. This is being accomplished through closures of salmon fishing near river mouths during peak steelhead runs, regulation of salmon gillnets to be used at depths below the level where steelhead swim, and spot closures to all fishing when steelhead are present in rivers. They are also working to cut down interception on the high seas by purse seiners and long-liners.

It's too early to know if the programs are working, but regardless of the cooperation between all these sectors and agencies there is one additional condition over which Canada has no control: Again, according to the BC Recreational Fisheries Advisory Council, the Alaskan commercial fishery is quite probably killing five times more Skeena and Dean steelhead as the BC commercial fishery did, as well as an equal amount of Skeena River coho...which as mentioned are now in even more trouble than steelhead! The exact reasons why this is so are unknown, but there are far more southern coast fish in those waters than previously. This web just keeps getting more and more tangled doesn't it?

For all that is known about steelhead, virtually nothing has been learned about the ocean migrations of coastal cutthroat—or if they even migrate. Most information indicates anadromous cutthroats remain in the estuaries of rivers where they entered the ocean, while other members of this species *Salmo clarki* stay in freshwater their entire lives, some being found as far inland as the continental divide. An aboriginal species if ever there was one.

Their original range included nearly all streams and lakes that connect with the Pacific Ocean, but cutthroat are so prone to over-fishing and their home streams so polluted, the present population is considerably fragile. Some streams and estuaries along the northern BC coast and in the Queen Charlotte Islands still have reasonably healthy numbers of good-sized fish— though none begin to approach their 40 pound land-locked monster cousins, the Lahontan cutthroat that once migrated up the Truckee River between Pyramid Lake, Nevada and Lake Tahoe. But that again is another story.

The Feed Awareness Factor

Knowing about the food salmon eat is such an important aspect of open ocean fly fishing that rather than revealing methods of finding them sporadically within the text I feel an open, more condensed discussion makes sense. And since I didn't know exactly where to place it, it seemed logical here before we get out on the water.

Whenever you search for salmon the single most significant factor in finding them is to find their feed. In an area that seems to have endless acres of baitfish, squid, shrimp and other forage, salmon won't be difficult to locate if they are around. But there are intervals when every place you hit seems barren. At times like that it is necessary to ignore the electronics on your boat and hunt fish the old fashion way...by using nature.

Knowing local conditions such as migration routes and places where schools of bait and salmon should be at specific times of the year are an obvious advantage, but sometimes they aren't where they should be because a natural or man-made environmental calamity occurred, or storms or other weather deviations altered their course, or climatic conditions like El Niño changed things...or a variety of other reasons. In that case, just as if you were in totally unfamiliar surroundings, locating salmon means covering miles of water searching for promising reefs and rock points, kelp beds, tidal currents, shallow banks, dropoffs or underwater structures that traditionally hold fish. If that fails, short of just running into a school somewhere by chance or hearing about a hot spot, there are certain things you can look for that will improve the likelihood of finding salmon.

The most reliable gauge is sea bird activity. I carry a pair of binoculars in my boat to scan the horizon for gulls and diving birds. A hoard of these whirling and dipping and diving to the water at a particular spot will indicate feed, and while such a show doesn't always mean salmon, it nearly always means baitfish (it could also mean a commercial fishing boat has thrown out fish entrails, or a cruise ship has passed by and dumped its garbage!). These binges don't usually last long in one place so hustle and get out there.

Determine which direction the school is moving by watching the birds and stay off to one side. There is no set rule about whether to cast ahead, into, or behind a baitfish school. Sometimes you see fish slashing across the top of the water which usually indicates coho. Chinook seem to stay below and behind the school, so if there is no apparent big-fish action on top, let your fly go deeper. If larger predator fish are feeding on the bait school you might also discover they are dog sharks, rockfish, cod or even halibut.

Many times your boat will put the bait school down soon after you arrive or the action just dwindles. Birds fly off a little distance and settle down on the water, or they might scatter. If you don't hit fish, sit quietly and wait for a few minutes. It shouldn't take long for the birds to locate the school and start up again. You can sometimes follow a school for a couple of hours this way and enjoy good action if salmon are around. If you get impatient and start running around in circles trying to find the school on your locator you might well put it down for good.

Other times you might see birds hovering just above the water or moving along in a stop-and-go sequence and not diving down. In this situation they can see bait flashing far down below and are waiting for the school to be forced to the surface. Petrals and small Bonaparte gulls are especially perceptive at this game and although there might only be one or two birds initially, if baitfish break the surface it won't be long until herring gulls and other sea birds will come from everywhere...particularly if there is a shortage of baitfish in the area. Whenever you see birds that seem to all be flying in one direction with a purpose, take a good look...even follow along. They have fantastic eyesight and hearing and will nearly always show you the way to a good feed.

Another reliable method of locating baitfish is to watch for diving birds. Sometimes there are large rafts of divers of all types—murres, auklets, puffins, loons, etc.—all working and creating quite a commotion. Small pigeon guillemots are masters at locating bait out in deep water, and whenever I see even one or two of these little guys working I always head over to check them out. Sit back and watch what they come up with. They bring their catch to the surface and a pair of binoculars will let you see the type and size of bait. In this situation if you can't see bait at or near the top use your locator to find the school. Often you will be out over deep water and bait will be down 40-feet or more which means using deepline techniques described elsewhere.

If the bait school down below doesn't seem to be moving or appears to be fairly uncondensed as you view it on your locator screen, chances are there are no predator fish working it. Often you see a large school of bait in what we call a "haystack." It will appear on your screen exactly as the name implies and may extend 30- or 40-feet from the top to the bottom of the school. If only a few diving birds are evident, they won't disturb this kind of school too much.

A large number of diving birds, a wildly scattered school with "holes" or dense separated clusters down below tells a different story, however. These are being hammered...probably by the birds that drew you there, but also possibly by salmon. This same action with the bait school at the surface is a sure indicator the school has been forced up, again, probably by the birds present, but always stop and give it a few casts.

A churning bait school with no birds around will mean only one thing...predator fish, and out over deep water chances are good they will be salmon. Unless you are having spectacular success at the spot you are, be aware of what is happening around you and always go where you see activity.

It's great when things are happening that you can *see* but what about when there is no surface activity? Besides turning on your locator and covering acres of water, there are a couple of things you can do by turning to your senses. (I usually get funny looks when I describing these, but bear with me. They work!)

One is to look for "nervous" water. Large schools of baitfish can actually cause water to become bumpy-nervous when they move en-masse just under the surface. This phenomenon can only be seen on flat calm water. From a distance it might appear as a dark spot, or an area of ripples, but whenever something different is happening at one location, give it a look.

Another event to look for is "fizzy" water. When schools of baitfish begin to rise from deep water upwards to a more shallow depth to feed or seek more comfortable temperatures or better oxygenated levels, they release tiny bubbles from their air bladders as they rise. These hit the surface just like carbonated soda water. You can actually see them glistening from a distance, and up close you can hear them fizz. Honest! Again, the water has to be fairly calm to notice this, but even in choppy water you can sometimes see it if you know what you are looking at. Clearly when this situation occurs, the larger the school the more bubbles will be evident.

Baitfish schools very often go right to the bottom and lay there. I have seen "bumps" on flat bottoms on my finder over 100-feet down that I was able to recognize as baitfish from it spreading or compacting as I watched. When they start moving up and you see air bubbles fizzing to the top then you know you've found a hot spot.

Once in awhile if conditions are right you can also smell baitfish, especially herring...and sometimes even spring salmon. In this case, follow your nose to the source. I have a native Indian friend who feels this is how some diving birds locate their feed. Upwelling currents from deeper water carry scent to the surface. He's very good at it, but I must admit my nose just isn't as tuned as his, though I definitely have smelled fish and then motored to an area where I was then able to find baitfish on my sounder.

There are many natural happenings that go on in the ocean—and indeed everywhere in nature—that we often fail to recognize even when they're right in front of us. Learn to "tune in" to anything that is unusual or different and investigate it. Your success will improve and so will your enjoyment of the hunt.

SUMMARY

This might be the only nice thing I will say about the commercial fishing fleet, but despite increased catches of sockeye, pink and chum salmon, DFO evidence indicates the incidental kill by the commercial fishery of Chinook, coho and steelhead has declined in the last few years because of efforts by commercial people to consider their impact on untargeted species. This news, coupled with reports that the roe-herring fishery is coming under better control, and that the forest industry is finally attempting to be accountable for their role in fisheries habitat reduction—along with the notion they might not be the main monsters in this story when natural climatic influences are factored in—gives this old heart a slight surge.

The people-impact is another story. I continue to hope we will change what is happening from our ceaseless human encroachment, but hope becomes less and less every year as stocks of coho, steelhead and cutthroat continue to decline. Federal agencies tell us about no net loss of salmon stocks they are charged with managing—and in fact there are claims of net increases—but since inventory of what we had to begin with was never taken, it's just talk. And provincial agencies simply put steelhead and cutthroat on "catch and release" programs and feel they have accomplished their management duties. I sure do believe in catch and release, but stocks keep sliding. Meanwhile, the inevitability of it all seems to have prompted some of us to give up, sit home and make babies instead of fighting bureaucrats. Granted, it's more fun, but when the battle is forgotten...then what? The truth is, it's getting very close to that time when there is no "what."

I hope plodding through my very brief and monumentally incomplete chronicle of the plight of salmonids along our west coast hasn't been too annoying or distressing. You bought this book to learn how to *catch* salmon in the ocean, not be subjected to my emotions and opinions about what is wrong with the system. But the fact is, something is *gravely* wrong and if it isn't corrected—or at least acknowledged and alternative plans considered—it won't matter how much you learn, there won't be salmon to catch.

Even the glimmer of promise for the future that I mention is frustrating because nothing under the control of mankind seems to be improving the fishery situation. There is dialogue from the right sources now, which is more than there has been, but they only repeat what we want to hear.

I wish *I* had the solutions. I *believe* I understand what's wrong. I think that part is becoming more obvious. As long as government bureaucrats serve only the dominant few (read: most imperious lobby groups) to the detriment of the many (read: us) time will advance until there are no clean streams, rivers, oceans, or wild fish. Combine these conditions with the human encroachment factor and naturally occurring adverse impacts, and again, then what? Overwhelming remorse.

There *is* ecstasy out there. I've found it, wallowed in it, exploited it, recognized it, and finally I have savored it. My passionate desire is that I have presented enough information and emotion to make you want to find it for yourself which will then prompt you to do all you can to be a conservator to the wasteful and destructive use of what is left.

What I write from here on is purely from my heart. I hope it won't be fantasy a generation from now.

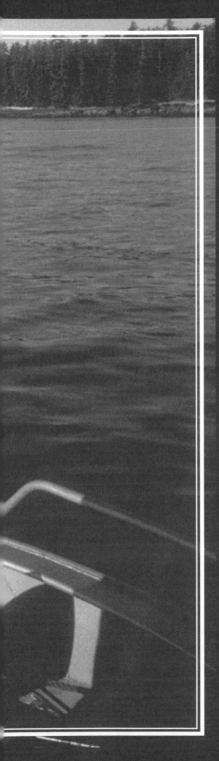

TWO

QUEEN CHARLOTTE ISLANDS, B.C.

HAIDA GWAII

Since my first trip here in the late 1960s the Queen Charlottes have held my heart. Timeless even today, this archipelago that sits on the edge of the Continental Shelf off the west coast of British Columbia and the Alaska panhandle is recorded on maps and charts as Queen Charlotte Islands, but natives there have known them as Haida Gwaii—roughly translated "Home of the Haida People"— for more than ten thousand years. Both are simply labels for one of the most beautiful and special places on earth.

Despite the usual questionable logging practices and a relentless exploitation of the ocean in some areas, there seems to be an almost limitless abundance of life in Haida Gwaii. Massive old-growth forests are haven to concentrated populations of Sitka blacktails (transplanted around 1900), huge ravens and some of the world's largest black bears. Crabs, prawns, shrimp and scallops crowd the bays. Dense beds of clams of every variety stretch for miles along clean, white beaches, and bald eagles and the world's healthiest population of peregrine falcons perch in trees and along rock cliffs and outcrops, watching for an easy meal.

Off shore, herring, needlefish (sand lance), squid and krill feed swarms of gulls, murres, pigeon guillemots, auklets, ancient and marbled murrelets, tufted puffins and, of course, predatory fish. It is a stopoff for all five species of Pacific salmon, migrating whales, exotic sharks and the occasional sunfish (that drift in with El Niño), and home to giant halibut and countless species of bottomfish. On the rocks are colonies of stellar sea lions, harbor seals, and northern fur seals. To be present in this world of the Haida is to step into what surely must be—and has always been—one of God's most bountiful places. It is truly overwhelming.

I first came to these islands on a photography assignment. Raw, primitive, they were still to be discovered by sports fishers and tourists then. I left with some new values and an immense respect for the Haida people and this incredible place...and a vision of world-class fly fishing potential. More people come here now and industry keeps up its relentless march against the resources, but nothing has dissuaded my first impressions.

HAIDA PEOPLE

Although the emphasis throughout Haida Gwaii principally is on fishing—especially for salmon and halibut—one is compelled to reflect on the pervasiveness of Haida culture, the result of literally thousands of years of continuous occupation of these islands.

Kung, a long-abandoned village site at the mouth of Naden Harbor, has been reliably dated back to 2500-BC by anthropologists from University of British Columbia and known to be built on top of several other settlements. Though now there are only overgrown logs and a few mortuary poles, the place has a mystical quality and sense of antiquity rarely experienced elsewhere. Freely sharing the copious abundance provided by nature gave countless generations of Haidas a rich and stable lifestyle...until smallpox and measles, brought by Europeans almost two centuries ago, decimated over 85 percent of the estimated 6,000 population in a few short years. Entire clans were eliminated, along with their specialized knowledge and unique cultural elements. In 1915 there were only 588 Haida Indians known to exist.

Today, nearly 2,000 descendants of the original population are concentrated in two small settlements: Old Masset at the north end of Graham Island—largest of the 150 islands here—and Skidegate at the south end. These modern Haida are attempting to revive their culture and, from what I have seen in recent years, they are having success. At Kiusta, on the northwestern point of Graham Island, a new longhouse stands in sharp contrast to the dim outlines in moss where ancient totems and longhouses once stood. Across a narrow peninsula facing the open ocean, three more new longhouses grace pristine beaches at Taa'lung'slung. Obviously projects like these undertaken in 1993 will attract individuals longing to experience one of north America's oldest and most unique cultures. It will also provide a tremendous opportunity for the Haida Nation to share their customs and culture with the world.

SALMON ALLOTMENT

In 1985 the U.S./Canada Pacific Salmon Treaty came into existence over concerns for dwindling stocks. A total of 230,000 Chinook salmon were allocated to the Canadian North Coast fishery, an area from the northern tip of Vancouver Island to the U.S. border in Alaskan waters; 210,000 were portioned to commercial trollers and the net fishery, and the remaining 20,000 were designated as a buffer in the (unlikely?) event of over-fishing. Because the take of Chinooks up to 1985 by the recreational sports fishery in northern waters was insignificant it was not considered in the Treaty, nor was the minimal native food fishery. Explosive growth in full-service destination fishing lodges—especially on the Queen Charlottes—has dramatically changed that, however.

If the annual allocation of Chinooks to Canada was exceeded in any year, the overage was to be "paid back" the following year through reduced commercial catch. In 1990, Canada's Department of Fisheries and Oceans calculated 5,600 sports fishermen killed over 20,000 Chinook salmon. By 1993 recreational catch figures had risen to 40,500, with numbers expected to continue to increase as that fishery expands. As a result, the sports fishery was recently given their own quota of 42,000 Chinooks, reducing the commercial quota to 188,000 plus any unused portion of the sports catch. The total annual Chinook harvest allowance is therefore being maximized with both the commercial fishing industry and the sports fishery responsible for maintaining their own quotas. The fast-growing sports user group is viewed as a threat to commercial fishing livelihoods, but for now at least there is a peace-of-sorts.

One interesting side note is the average revenue per fish generated by the different groups: according to the BC Sports Fishery Advisory Council, for every single salmon caught at the 25 lodges in northern waters sports fishers pay $249.00 compared to an average return of $18.00 per salmon to commercial fishermen in those same waters. If those figures are applied to Chinook salmon only—which is what most sports fishers seek—the figure jumps to $503.00 per fish paid by the recreational fishery. Sports fishers killed an average of 38,000 Chinook in northern waters in the last five years while the commercial fleet killed an average of 192,000 in the same time frame.

Right now the recreational sports fishery spends a hair under $1,000,000,000. (that's *billion!*) a year pursuing salmon in British Columbia saltwater, while the commercial industry generated a total of $168,000,000. (This 1991 figure, of course, fluctuates annually with the rise and fall of salmon market prices while the sports figure keeps going up every year.) These figures were taken from the DFO *Fact Sheet—1992*, and from a 1994 BC Sports Fishery Advisory Council publication. Makes one wonder why so much attention is paid to the commercial fishing sector when the sports fishing sector spends nearly six times more money to catch only one fifth the number of fish. Of course, I'll no doubt be taken to task regarding these figures since every economist seems to have a different method of measuring and equating such values, but just remember the 60-some DFO mandarin-type bureaucrats who must continue to justify their salaries in Ottawa and it will give you some idea why the commercial fishery sector is held so dear.

Sickened by uncontrolled harvest in both ocean and forest by "outsiders," the Haida Nation has also begun to take active steps to protect Haida Gwaii and its resources through aboriginal title. Many sports fishing lodges and commercial fishermen support their efforts, but a lack of clear goals, limited money and manpower, and a divided leadership has severely hampered native conservation efforts so far in the 90s. As a result, every user group continues to take all that the law allows and conflict seems inevitable. Hopefully, by the time this is in print, Canadian federal and provincial agencies—and the Haida Nation—will have the problems under control.

Meanwhile, time may be running out for the main object of all the squabbling: Canada's last remaining runs of giant wild Chinook salmon. Before heading across Hecate Strait and up the Skeena River system to their home rivers, these fish spend time in historic feeding grounds around the northern Queen Charlottes where they are the target of sports fishers from around the world. Such magnificent fish, frequently in the Tyee class (over 30 pounds) and sometimes reaching 60 pounds, are irreplaceable. Not even the great salmon runs in Alaska rivers compare because these are reachable, touchable in their wildest natural ocean habitat. Though it may sound redundant, when these particular stocks of huge Chinooks are gone, the species will disappear forever. Conservation measures—however late—aimed at all users need to be undertaken now.

CHASING CHINOOK

Those concerns notwithstanding, waters off the northern Queen Charlottes offer the most exciting Chinook and coho fly fishing one can experience anywhere on the west coast. Difficult to reach and expensive, the results—as the adage goes—definitely justify the means!

My most recent trip was better than any previous. Three of us flew to Sandspit from Vancouver, BC in mid-July, and transferred to a small sea plane for the final 15 minute hop. Schools of Chinook begin arriving in May to fatten up for spawning runs in August, and by July they are at a peak, joining resident schools to create an immense mass of fish that covers the entire northern end of the islands. Such abundance belies the tenuous structure of this fishery, but we weren't there to kill. Instead we wanted to test vulnerability...our own and that of the salmon.

Our base was Queen Charlotte Lodge, located in Naden Harbor. One of more than a dozen destination lodges in the region reached only by plane or boat, this magnificent new log structure, built in 1992, is in harmony with the environment and has the blessings of the Haida people. I have been fortunate to stay at some of the most exclusive fishing resorts in North America (and a couple of the worst!) and this new facility is truly among the finest in every way. "First class" is measured by several standards and Queen Charlotte Lodge has them all. Nothing is overlooked or left to chance, from care of rooms to outstanding food to great boats and gear to top rate personnel.

Because airplane space is limited, fly fishers can only bring a couple of outfits, and for anyone accompanying who does not fly fish, the lodge provides everything they will need. This is an outstanding operation, and though writers frequently receive "gratis" trips, this wasn't one. I paid the whole shot so my comments are from the depths of my bank account. Anyway, everything costs money. I have a fortune tied up in rods, reels, lines, clothes and enough different boats, rafts, kick-boats and float tubes for every part of my body, so why not spend a little more and go to a place where the fish are so big and eager I won't have to fantasize? And no, I can't afford it! But hey, if I wait until I can I won't be physically (or mentally) able.

Within an hour of our afternoon arrival, we were stuffed with assorted sandwiches, salads and seafood and sent waddling off to be outfitted in the requisite commercial flotation suits and boots. We were assigned a custom, center-console aluminum boat with a 50 hp outboard, and following orientation from staff, we loaded our gear and headed out of the harbor for the two-mile run to one of our favorite areas. All three of us have extensive ocean boating experience, and because of familiarity with the area from previous trips we opted to go on our own. Guides are available (and recommended for at least the first day), and the lodge has two high-speed boats that constantly make rounds among the guest fleet with extra gear, refreshments, advice and to provide an added margin of safety.

Even so, the weather and water in this region demand respect. They can kill you in a blink...a state I constantly flirt with in lesser situations. I can't count the number of times I've wailed, "God, please just let me make it through this and I promise I won't ever do it again." But as soon as the fear is gone I get as careless as ever, a trait my fishing partners have often left me to aspire to on my own. Out here very bad things can happen instantly. Don't screw around.

The first kelp bed we stopped at yielded a perfect 23 pound Chinook that ambushed my fly under a motionless sea and flat gray sky. An excellent—in truth, exceptional—beginning to what would be an eventful week for salmon and some personal evaluations. Chinook are *not* that easy and I don't want to give the impression they are. This one was in the right mood and in the right place, and we were both surprised.

I had rigged my favorite 9-foot, 9-weight G. Loomis IMX graphite with a 350-grain lead-core shooting taper, 100-feet of Cortland running line, and a nine-foot leader tapered to 20-pound-test plus three-feet of 12-pound tippet. My reel was an old model 578 Pflueger Supreme backed with 300-yards of 30-pound Dacron. Bob Jones, Canada's renowned fishing writer who lives in Courtenay, BC had tied a dozen Firecracker flies for me. On a 2X extra-strong hook tied with pearlescent Mylar tubing garnished with Krystal Flash, Firecrackers are the deadliest flies I have ever found for salmon. I picked a size 6 bent to roll in the water like a wounded herring when retrieved.

Chinook like a slow spin, cohos like it faster, and as long as it reasonably matches bait size and color fish will take it. Truth be known, they will hit just about any fly if conditions are right, like when they are feeding. For that reason I don't change flies too often; rather, I *hunt* for feeding fish. In Haida Gwaii, unlike in other areas, Chinooks often feed throughout the day instead of just at dawn or dusk or when the tides turn.

Normally several hours of thrashing per hookup are required for Chinooks. This one came on the third cast along the kelp. I had laid out about 80-feet of line and because the water was fairly shallow—maybe 30-feet—I didn't wait for the lead-core to take the fly down before I started my slow two-foot strips. The hit was typically Chinook, a soft tap, then nothing. I pointed my rod and stripped quickly until I felt resistance, then set up. The first run was long and hot, with a series of spectacular jumps that I was helpless to control. But it was a wide open clear track and I had 300-yards of backing. A half-hour later, with the best sequences safely on video, we released a sterling-bright, hefty female. There wasn't another boat in sight. Perhaps a half-mile out from us a throng of screeching gulls were working on a bait school, and nearby on an outcropping of rocks several sea lions dozed. Amazing.

We drifted back to the kelp and cast awhile, then motored on up to Bird Rock I, another favorite spot. Only a few bottomfish answered our probes. But that was okay...the pressure was off. I'd done my job. Tomorrow was another day.

Back at the lodge, our first day—and in fact every day—ended with a sip or two of good single-malt scotch and a sumptuous soak in the steaming outdoor hot tub. Here, even in July and dressed warmly, a day on the ocean can be bone chilling. As the numbness left my body I wondered how the Haida had combated this kind of cold.

In the days that followed our schedule became quite civilized: breakfast at 5:30 or 6:00 a.m., fishing by 7:00, lunch on the *M.V. Driftwood*—a 110-foot ship that anchors near the fishing grounds each day to provide a warm, quiet break for guests—then back to the lodge for evening cocktails and dinner by about 9:30. If this trip was measured only by the food and service it would still rate positively excellent! But we weren't there to put on any more weight.

Bird Rocks I and II became our daily starting points, and they always paid off with coho or pinks, and on special occasions—like that first afternoon— a Chinook, or some other surprise. On the third morning we were delayed by heavy inland fog. We confidently started out of the harbor using a compass, but our navigational skills were not good. Our boat made a gradual looping left turn and ran aground. Fortunately we were able to stop the motor prior to grunging into the gravel bottom and nothing but our combined pride was hurt (no one else ever heard that story...until now). By the time we got untangled and out on the water a bright sun was high above the island. We weren't used to that. The sea was glass calm with low swells, and we could see all the way out to Langara Island...a dangerous thing because it aroused the urge to explore beyond the boundary set by the lodge. And it was my turn to "drive" that day.

Clearing it with one of the lodge guides we cruised west around Cape Naden point and along the shoreline...rugged, rocky, heavily treed with original growth spruce and firs, past kelp beds, basking sea lions, bald eagles and endless piles of driftwood thrown high by storms and surf. An hour later we were at Pillar Rock, more than halfway to Langara. Boats from other lodges were concentrated in the bay and several people were playing fish on long mooching rods favored by BC guides. Similar to saltwater fly outfits, mooching rigs are long, limber 10- or 11-foot rods fitted with large capacity single-action reels and 300- to 600-yards of monofilament. 'Light' 15 to 20-pound-test leaders, 1/2 to 2-ounce weights, and two single or treble hooks baited with either cut-plug herring or small whole herring, slowly trolled or lobbed out and stripped in, is deadly for Chinook and coho. It is not unusual to see a hooked fish run out 200-yards or more of line, jump or roll, and then take out some more. Big fish on this supple tackle are great fun and it's as close to fly fishing as bait fishermen can get. Other than the bait part I don't have a problem with this type of fishing. It lets people who have never hooked a salmon before have the thrill of a lifetime and gives the fish a better than equal chance. I suspect it also converts the occasional person over to fly fishing when they learn how much fun it is using single-action reels.

Although we had each hooked at least one Chinook, so far only the one had been landed. Taking care to stay well away from boats with fish on we moved through the pack looking for bait on our finder. At 30-feet, a big school lit up the scope. As our boat drifted across, Doug and George cast back towards the front edge of the school, giving maximum slack to let their flies go deep. On the first strip George had a solid strike that he missed. Then another. Missed. Finally he set the hook...into a 5 pound black rockfish. Doug had the same result. Fun, but embarrassing with everyone watching...kind of like hooking a bluegill when everyone else is catching 10 pound bass. "Yeah, man, those fly fisher guys sure do have the secret don't they...yuk-yuk." Sheepish grins.

Back over the bait school. Long casts. Sink deep. Bang, bang, bang, rock-fish for all. More chagrin. Aim the other way. Cast, cast. Rest. We were getting frustrated. Salmon were there. Two or three hookups in other boats proved that, and we were right on the bait school. Think, Jim, think.

"Let's go to the back of the school and try," George's reasoning was the bait was moving "upstream" into the slight tidal current and salmon would be following, picking up injured herring that fell out after being pounded by all the predator fish and diving birds feeding on them.

While we were deciding what to do Doug had cast behind the boat and his line had gone to the bottom. I hadn't noticed. As I put the motor in gear his line lifted and almost immediately he had a vicious strike. This time he set the hook into a monster Chinook that missiled out of the water and then headed deep. "Not fair hooked," yelled George, "you were trolling." "Just turn on the camera..."

After some heavy give and take, Doug's fish was in the net, a quivering tor-pedo over 20 pounds. Applause broke out from boats all around us, obvious-ly pleased that we were finally able to pull it off and join their exalted ranks. We quickly snapped a couple of still pictures and then cheers became aston-ished gasps when Doug released it on the side of our boat with the most spec-tators. One guide remarked, "The dogfish (sharks) will have a good feast tonight." A sophisticated, enlightening comment if ever I heard one. Kill them all, Dufuss, and see how long your job lasts. Impress your dudes. "Don't say it, Jim," George warned. I mentally took note of the lodge name on the side of his boat, fantasizing a visit there in the dark of night dressed in my best gang-land slaying outfit and turning the place into rubble. I was mad!

Suddenly I wanted to get away from that crowd. I mean, what's the use. Catch and release didn't bring back customers intent on hauling home a hun-dred pounds of salmon meat, or guides who wanted to be top gun. Not fair to say of all guides, certainly, but this bunch sure didn't fit my description of an elite crew. While we were sorting things out after releasing our fish, two more were hauled in and clubbed. More cheers. I'm sorry, but we sure as hell can't blame declining salmon stocks all on the commercial guys and loggers.

As we were leaving, a wonderful thing happened. At first I wasn't sure if I had conjured up the vision or if someone else was just on my same wave length. A small fleet of boats, including several outboards of various descriptions and an old black and red wooden trawler, headed right for the pack of lodge boats. With outriggers flared and cannon balls down the trawler drove right through the middle, snagging lines and cutting off at least one rod with a fish on as boats scattered in all directions. Two of the maverick outboards closed in on lodge boats and followed about 20-feet behind them as they trolled, sitting over their lines. No cheers now. Just yelling, obscenities, flipping off. We couldn't believe it. What delicious chaos! At least I thought so at the time.

These guides had obviously been through the program before. As a group they upped lines and headed for lodges on Langara, quickly outrunning the intruders. Without waiting to see if we would be next we pointed east and didn't look back. We needn't have worried. We learned later Queen Charlotte Lodge was one of a few lodges on the "approved" list the Haida natives were not targeting for aggressive activity as one of the ways to fight against wanton exploitation of salmon resources by outsiders. We were the good guys. I had to remember to ask our host about it.

This was the third time that summer similar incidents had occurred. Each time the Royal Canadian Mounted Police marine unit was called in to help control the situation, but from what we saw there wasn't much to control. The "attack" was ill-planned and not very sustained. Still, such civil disobedience serves to disrupt the comfort of lodge guests and was becoming a thorn as it were. A close friend of mine in the RCMP, directly involved in the disputes, told us that while these incidents on the water hadn't yet posed any real danger, sustained activity surely would. One or two of the lodges had hotheads who threatened to retaliate if it didn't stop, so the police were called in and two or three charges laid against native leaders.

The conflict over recreational fishermen killing too many Chinooks is coming from two groups concerned over the increase presently estimated at 40,000 in the northern fishery: First, from commercial fishermen who regard the Queen Charlottes—and in particular the Langara Island area—as the "last frontier" of salmon fishing that they must fight for if they wish to see their livlihood continue. So far the commercial group has not become militant, but those in position to know say it is only a matter of time. The second group are the native Haida. It was their feeble attempt to assert aboriginal fishing rights in the only option they see open that we witnessed. As enthusiastic as I might have felt during the heat of the action, in reality that is not the way to go about getting something constructive accomplished. People could have been hurt, and may yet be, and all it does is expand the potential for more conflict. Guys like me cheering them on doesn't help.

Instead, several lodges, and indeed even local commercial fishermen, have begun "funding" the Haida in their efforts to preserve the Chinook fishery, even though there is no clear cut native agenda for allocating monies received. When I heard that comment it became obvious why boats with the Queen Charlotte Lodge name and logo are left alone. I don't know if I approve or disapprove of this seemingly blatant "protectionism" scheme, but if it is helping preserve Chinook who am I to criticize efforts. According to the Canadian Department of Fisheries and Oceans' own records, the recreational sports fishery spends nearly six times the amount annually to catch salmon in British Columbia waters as commercial fishermen bring in, so it sure makes sense that the lodges would want to contribute to the preservation of Chinook salmon!

That night over dinner, our host filled us in on how he hopes the groups will resolve the discord. He didn't want some of the specific things he talked about to be repeated, so I will honor that, but in general he sees the number of lodges, and hence the volume of recreational fishermen, being restricted as well as cutbacks to both the sports and commercial catch of Chinooks. I know from experience that some personnel here believe in limiting the number of fish killed by their guests, and I naturally agree. There is certainly nothing wrong with taking a fish home for eating and showing, but after a couple of glasses of wine I got off on a whole tangent—as I usually do—about only killing "runts" (fish under 20 pounds) rather than trophies so the genetic pool stays strong. Afterwards, I felt there was genuine brotherly understanding around the table as we got into our fourth bottle of wine.

HALIBUT QUEST

Next morning we were to fish with a Haida commercial fisherman for halibut, and since halibut are meat-eaters we weren't expecting to fly fish. Charlie, our guide-for-a-day, showed up in a classic turn-of-the-century 40-foot trawler. It had been painted dozens of times over the years, one coat on top of the other, the latest being white with black accents. Long, bare, hand-carved cedar outriggers, folded neatly up along each side of the cabin gave it a top-heavy appearance, and the cannonballs, trolling lines, and planers were neatly arranged, each in its place. There was no mistake what this boat was all about. We wouldn't use his trolling gear, of course, but the various ropes, wires and pulleys would definitely limit any thoughts we had about fly casting. I took along one fly outfit anyway just on the off chance.

As we turned out of the harbor a northwest wind whistled through the rigging and healed the old round-bottomed boat slightly to starboard. "Oh, this is going to be *wonderful*," George sniped. "It'll be rock and roll. Hope you land dudes don't get sick. I'll have to eat all the lunches."

"That reminds me," said Charlie, "I brought along some Haida candy to snack on. Octopus marinated in oolichan oil." (Also spelled oolachan, eulachon and probably a couple other ways, oolichans are small smelt-like fish. They are so oily it is said one could be strung with a wick and burned like a candle, giving rise to yet another name, candlefish...). Oh, man. Sudden head-rush. I have a very strong stomach, but that thought, combined with the smell of diesel exhaust swirling around us, and the boat heaving against the waves... I asked Charlie about the feeding habits of halibut to take my mind off the vision sloshing around in my mind.

"Everyone thinks halibut stay in deep water, and many do, but here we try to fish them shallow. Maybe 90- or 100-feet. Their main diet is horseneck clams, so anywhere there is sand. They go along the bottom and nip off the tips of the clam necks sticking up." Get out! I didn't believe that, *at all* (I would later have to eat these thoughts which would be much better than the alternative).

About two miles east along the shoreline towards Masset, Charlie slowed and came about into the wind which had picked up considerably. We were 200-yards off a solid rock shore and all crowded into the small cockpit area at the back of the boat. Including Charlie! "Who's driving the boat?"

"Drop in here. It's about 50-feet. Sandy. Good spot!" Pitch. Roll. I needed a safety belt.

We had taken three mooching outfits from the lodge each rigged for bait fishing with 2-ounce weights and two single size 3/0 hooks. I decided to let the other two guys start while I took pictures. They baited up with octopus pieces (not the oolichan stuff, that was for humans), dropped down and George's line barely hit bottom when he hooked up. Dead weight. Pump, lift, pump, lift. Gaff. About a 35 pounder. Wham. Doug had one. Same scene, except when his got to the surface there was a second halibut with it. I dropped my camera, stripped out some line, and whipped out my Firecracker. Right under his nose. "Come on, suck it in..."

When I set up it was like someone had tied a five pound cannonball to the end of my line! The fish went straight to the bottom. The only experience I can relate it to was hooking a rock. My 9-weight rod is sturdy, but it was not made to lift 35 or 40 pounds straight up. I have landed sailfish weighing over 100 pounds in Mexico with less effort (though on heavier rods). With the trawler pitching and diving and rolling, this was not fun! I just couldn't do anything. "Charlie, I only have 12-pound-test leader here."

"Hold on, hold on...I'll show you something." He moved the boat about 50-yards into the pounding waves as I let out line. "Now lift." The angle forced the fish's head up and it planed right to the surface. Neat trick! He backed down on it as I held pressure and reeled, and it was gaffed aboard...not as easily as I make it sound. I wish I could report it was an exciting fight and that halibut are now on my list of ten most sought-after fish, but we all know better! What *is* exciting is what one can do when brought into the boat green. All the stories about broken boat seats, rods, legs, etc., are undoubtedly true. These primitive creatures are incredibly hard to kill and have been known to "come back to life" an hour after being clubbed and put away. Charlie dispatched this one efficiently with a couple swipes of his filleting knife, then tossed it up on his cleaning board and, with what I'm certain was a smirk, proceeded to gut it. A double scoop of severed clam necks spilled out onto the tray.

We called it quits after that and Charlie took us back. Along the way he pointed out a couple of long-abandoned shoreline village sites of his people, rock-lined canoe launches, and cedar trees used for totems or the giant dugout war canoes the Haidas were respected for among all Indian tribes in the Northwest. We never would have noticed on our own. Thanks, Charlie, it was truly a valuable and unforgettable experience.

SALTWATER CUTTHROAT

It was too rough to venture outside the sound so after lunch (we traded our bag lunches in on something *much* lighter!) we took our boat across Naden Harbor to a gravel bar to try for cutthroat. Tom Murray, a friend from Nanaimo, BC who was guiding that summer, discovered them in abundance all around the harbor (Tom also keeps himself well versed on various issues concerning salmonids here as well as Vancouver Island. He's a good contact). On a rising or falling tide cutts dimple the surface next to shore acting like young trout do everywhere.

Unfortunately we hadn't brought any light fly gear, but I put on my floating shooting taper and some 6-pound straight monofilament as a leader, and tied on one of Tom's Rolled Muddler Minnows...about a size 10. On my 9-weight rod I wouldn't feel much.

It was a blast. The little cutthroats came eagerly to almost every cast. I finally took off the butt section of my rod, restrung, put the reel in my pocket and just used the tip and 30-foot floating head. Much more fun! Some of the cutts weren't much bigger than my fly. Real trophies! And I landed one monster of 13-inches after a monumental test of man and material. No matter, I truly enjoyed the break. Even the part where I had to wade out up to my armpits to retrieve our boat that had drifted off with the incoming tide.

The cutthroat fishery here has great potential. Tom has taken them to 2 pounds and feels there are much larger ones waiting in stream and river mouths that feed the sound, and in creeks that surround the islands. I'll definitely have a light saltwater outfit with me next trip. It was great fun!

DEEP WATER CHINOOK

So far we'd done everything we set out to do. We each had landed a Chinook, several cohos, halibut, and more bottomfish than we could count. This day we would concentrate on Chinooks in deep water, a feat only the downrigger and mooching crowd were able to accomplish with any consistency. I have fished deep for salmon on many occasions—and I am reasonably proficient at it—but I have always had better results in the top 30- to 40-feet of water. In many regions, Chinook stay deep—90-feet or more—until they move up to feed, and that might only be "up" to the 50- or 60-foot level. In most regions we look for them on high or low slack tides, and in the hour both before and after, and then again right at daylight or dusk. Here, they were inshore right next to the kelp or chasing bait seemingly all the time. In May a 62-pound giant was hooked next to the kelp in barely 20-feet of water at Bird Rock II. Two hours and two miles later, it was netted—and killed!—even though the entire contest was recorded on video.

The northwest wind had lain down from our previous day's adventure, and the gray overcast had returned merging the glassy water and horizon into a vast, almost eerie endlessness. We felt very small out there. I unracked my Loomis IM6 Mega 12-weight and put on a 700-grain Deep Water Express head with a 9-foot tapered leader and about three feet of 20-pound tippet. For this program I tied on a 4-inch Improved Polar Herring fly (body of polar bear belly hair from a taxidermist friend, and blue/green Krystal Flash back, tied together at the hook bend leaving a short tail). It's a bitch to cast all that, so we decided only one of us at a time would fish.

Using our finder (Doug brought his portable Bottom Line unit; lodge boats aren't equipped with them) we located a wide rock ledge that sloped away from a huge flat in about 90-feet of water. It dropped off to over 300-feet in just a short distance. Well...we wanted *deep*. The screen showed some large fish suspended above the flat bottom that could be just about anything—sharks, salmon, lings, a school of rockfish...

Normally we would use a sinking-line method I have used in deep water for many years. After locating a bait school or fish on the locator and determining drift, lob the heavy shooting taper as far ahead of the boat as possible, strip out enough line to get down to the fish, then keep it there as the boat drifts over the spot. Using a heavy-duty Leisenring lift and drop technique— sometimes even letting out more line as the boat goes by—keep the fly at that level as long as possible. This method is also used by lure fishers, especially when there is a strong tide or wind. It has accounted for some outstanding results...(and just as often *no* results).

But in this instance, to save time and possible injury to Doug or George— or more probably to myself—instead of casting I stripped out about 120-feet of line behind the moving boat.

Line disappeared into the blackness. It took over three minutes to hit the 90-foot bottom and by then the boat had floated back. I let the line lay for a moment, then began lifting the rod tip slowly and reeling in on the down stroke as the boat moved by (once I got to the running line I planned to strip, but for now I didn't want a ball of Dacron backing around my feet). There was a very slight tide running and the wind remained calm...both are essential factors when using fly gear for this program.

"Something strange is going on here," my line had gone slack and I couldn't feel any resistance.

"Reel, reel!" There was urgency in George's tone. I didn't quite understand but I cranked. A huge Chinook rocketed through the surface about 50-feet behind us, winged the fly to one side, and crashed back down. Two more jumps and then only holes in the water where he had been. I should have recognized what was happening. In salt, Chinook will overtake a fly from behind or the side and softly mouth it. Sometimes one will shake its head, giving the telltale tap-tap of a Chinook-take, or, like this one did, it will continue swimming on the same course and if there is something out of the ordinary or it feels the hook it will hit afterburner and go for the surface. In either case the line will go slack indicating the fish is moving with the line. If you are in touch with your fly you'll recognize when that happens and strip quickly until you feel the fish and can set the hook. My senses were in nirvana with this one.

"Man, that was neat! So now we know they're down there." It was not difficult locating more fish at about the same 90-foot depth. George stepped up to bat and fired out about 80-feet of line—no small effort with such a heavy shooting system. He stripped out more running line and backing as the line fell towards the bottom. Six casts, one snag and one small lingcod and he wanted to rest. Tough work this deep water express stuff!

Doug was next, and like me he opted to let the line trail behind the moving boat for a distance, then stop and let it go down. Typical of our friend Doug's luck, the line didn't even get to the bottom when his rod bumped a couple of times and then straightened. "It's a spring, D (*spring* is the BC anomaly for Chinook, like *king*, or Jim Teeny's *chromer*), don't do what Crawford did." He reeled, caught up with it and set the hook. This one stayed deep and took short rips of line, pounding the rod with head shakes and tail sweeps. Then one long run and it came to the surface about 100-yards back. It looked huge even that far away. Then it was pump, reel, run, for another forty minutes. Finally in the net next to the boat we admired it. An immense male, deep and long, close to 40 pounds. It would be our best fish of the trip. "Boy, I'd sure like to keep him." George and I gave him *that* look and photographed the release.

We stayed over the drop-off for another half hour, but the tide began moving and a breeze picked up so we went off in search of other wonders. The deep water system doesn't always work, but when you find a situation like the one described—bait or fish in 40- to 100-feet of water, very light tide and no wind—give it a go.

Of Pinks and Coho

On our last afternoon two vast schools of coho and pink salmon arrived. They were moving everywhere as far as the eye could see, and anyone with a hook in the water caught fish. Action was fast and furious, and hoots and hollers echoed with every hookup. The guests were having a blast, but to the guides who baited their hooks and handled their fish, it was a pain. Big fish mean big tips. These were just a nuisance. Since this was no doubt one of the last feeding stops they would make before their biological clocks would trigger the spawning urge and they would stop eating and head for home rivers on the mainland, we wanted to get in on it.

I re-rigged to a floating line, tied a tiny black ballbearing swivel to the terminal end of my leader, and snapped on a small Firecracker. Yeah, I suppose it becomes a "lure" when you do that (in truth, what fly isn't?), but I wanted a fast-spin on the fly, and if I happened to hook a pink they roll so much the line would twist without the swivel.

This "hatch" was a no-brainer. It didn't matter which direction we cast, it wasn't very often one of us—or *all* of us—didn't have a fish on. Coho like a fast spinning retrieve and there wasn't anything subtle about their takes. Wham, then gonzo through the top almost in the same motion. Jump, rip, run. Slamming the boat, never stopping their headlong thrust. Slime, scales, half digested herring sticking there. Man. They ripped up our flies and our nerves...but what a way to go! All around 5 to 7 pounds, with the odd 8 or 9 pounder. *Hot* fish.

Coho are in this area all the time, and excellent runs come throughout the summer and fall. Sizes increase too. We were never there after July, but residents told us September can be awesome when big "northerns" roll in (more on northerns in a later section). Hope to find out about those in the Charlottes someday.

Three hours later we dropped our rods and motored over to the *M.V. Driftwood* to have something to eat. The RCMP's newest boat was there, a 60-foot, dual engine tunnel-hull that can hit over 30-knots. I can tell you it is damned impressive when moving at top speed. The rooster tail it throws is higher and longer than the boat! The three gendarmes aboard were on their way up to Langara to look into the row between natives and lodge boats we had seen. We kept tight lips. Beautiful boat though.

After lunch and war stories from guests who had been in the thick of the coho blood bath that morning, we headed back out to see just how big the school was. At least two miles off shore we got into a bird feeding-frenzy. Tiny two-inch current-year herring were everywhere and every predator for miles was in on the spread. We could see salmon 10-feet below us ripping through the feed. I didn't even cast, I just dropped my Firecracker over the side then got down on my knees and peered down into the water to watch. A pink about three pounds came out from under the boat and inhaled the softly spinning fly. I saw the whole thing, like in slow motion. I didn't even have to lift my rod, the fish did it all. As soon as it hit it began to twist and gyrate as pinks always do. Suddenly it streaked away in a long ten foot run. Whew. I pulled it towards the boat and the hook ripped out just as I reached for it. Soft mouth. "Let's get out of here."

Too late. Doug and George both hooked up. Twist, roll, spin. "Geez, they're like little sea rats." Typical George comment. Then he made the slurping noise Dr. Hannibal "The Cannibal" Lechter did when telling Clarice about dining on someone's liver while sipping "a lovely Chianti" in *Silence of the Lambs*. I guess you had to be there. Anyway, we were getting silly. It had been a long, beautifully fatiguing week, and this was a great windup.

SUMMARY

The last couple of days, before the coho-pink theater, and after some serious hunting, we connected with several more shallow-water Chinooks. George and Doug each took fish in the 30 to 40 pound class. I hooked a total of seven and only landed the one at the beginning of our trip. I was too heavy-handed, breaking off on the setup or getting my fingers in the way of running line, or letting them throw the fly at long distance (commonly known as forgetting to set the hook). I'd have let them go anyway, but it would have been rewarding to at least get some slime on my hands. Native culture states that man and nature must always be in balance. On this trip nature was way ahead of me. But that was OK.

On our last night while we sat in the hot tub soaking our cut and nicked fingers and bruised limbs, we relived every hookup until we were too weak to move. Pleasant exhaustion. Magnificent trip. I'll drink to that!

GETTTING THERE

Most lodges provide charter air service as part of their packages. There are also scheduled flights daily to Sandspit, Queen Charlotte Islands from Vancouver, BC and car rentals available by reservation if you only go to sightsee. As mentioned, lodges are only reachable by boat or plane. For a list of lodges on the Queen Charlottes, write: Ministry of Tourism—Parliament Buildings—Victoria, British Columbia V8V 1X4 and ask for their Accommodation and Travel Guide, or phone 1-800/663-6000.

You *could* drive there and tow your boat, but it's one wild trip. You would drive to Prince Rupert, BC (900 miles from Vancouver, B.C.) and catch a BC Ferry to Queen Charlotte City, then drive north to Masset and stay in a motel or camp. There is good fishing all over the north end of the islands, and elsewhere around them I'm sure...but I haven't had experience anywhere except Masset to Langara.

Anyone contemplating a trip here should obtain marine charts 3692—Queen Charlotte Islands, and 3895—Langara Island. Write Canadian Hydrographic Service, Department of Fisheries and Oceans, P.O. Box 6000, Sidney, BC V8L 4B2 and request their catalog of small craft charts for the Pacific Coast. Charts presently cost around $14.00 Canadian plus GST and shipping.

SALMON TO A FLY

THREE

NORTHERN VANCOUVER ISLAND

PORT MCNEILL, B.C.

$\mathcal{I}$t was late July and I was with two legendary fly fishers from Kamloops, Jack Shaw and Ralph Shaw, on our annual quest to northern Vancouver Island for salmon. We had arrived in the Port McNeill area just in time to wave at the biggest run of coho in several years as it moved south. They were expected to arrive in Campbell River, half-way down the inland side of the Island, in about a week or so. There was no way to intercept them until then.

Our base was Bauza Cove Camp and RV Park, located in a small bay adjacent to where Pacific water from Queen Charlotte Strait constricts and pushes into narrow Johnstone Strait. There are colossal rip tides here, and the sea life is astonishing: Gray and minke whales, pods of orcas (a.k.a. killer whales and blackfish), otters, sea lions, harbor seals, gulls and murres, and fish of every kind and size. The shoreline is solid-rock-rugged, no beaches or hiking trails, just stones and boulders worn smooth by centuries of pounding waves, slime-covered and cold even under bright sun. Back from the ocean is thick forest—fir and hemlock, cedars, some spruce and pine...the habitat of a timber-tough, carefree, outdoor-loving, have-a-beer, live-on-the-edge crowd. I love it up there. My kind of place.

On the floating dock sports-trollers were unloading boatloads of pink salmon averaging three to five pounds. Home canneries were cranked up in camp, and pans and pails heaped with chunks of fish were carried to waiting cookers. Every table had a stove with a pressure cooker and boxes of glass jars. Assembly lines. Mass production. I imagined every motor home and camper with a false floor or "special" gas tank to hide the plunder. Almost every license plate read Washington, Oregon, California, Idaho, California, California, Missouri(?). Canadians think this is why "their" salmon are disappearing. Amazing. A bottle of Cardhu, and later, heaping plates of our friend Bill's spaghetti with the appropriate garlic-cheese sourdough bread and we hardly noticed the Coleman stoves hissing long into the night.

SOCKEYE

Early mornings are often foggy and the water glass calm on northern Vancouver Island. That first morning we ran our boat ten miles out on Queen Charlotte Strait, stopping when we encountered hundreds of surface-feeding salmon extending far into the haze. Cast after cast produced nothing and someone finally remarked, "They must be sockeye!" Sockeye are the only salmon that "don't bite." Yet they were feeding on something and whatever it was could surely be matched with a fly pattern. I kneeled down and pulled in a cupped hand of tiny pinkish-transparent creatures, probably crustacean larvae (shrimp or krill), though I didn't have a clue. We went off to find more responsive subjects, but the sockeye intrigued me. Remembering the fun I'd had with them on Adams River years before I decided there had to be a way.

That night I made the rounds of every fisherman I knew to ask about sockeye. The answer was always the same, "Sockeye don't bite." Only Gordon Graham, owner of Bauza Cove Camp gave me any encouragement. He had occasionally hooked them on a small pink fly tied very sparsely and retrieved dead-slow. I jumped on his pattern and early the next morning we were back hitting on the school we'd encountered the day before. I got one bump before the sun burned through the fog and the school quit feeding. Disappointing, but it was a start.

The next winter I read everything I could find on this gentle salmon, and asked questions of anyone who showed even the slightest interest. I learned as juveniles they feed almost exclusively on so-called "pink feed"—aquatic invertebrates like zooplanktons and minute crustaceans—and must sometimes travel incredible distances to find sufficient quantities. Apparently they will also take more substantial feed—herring and needlefish fry, and shrimp—when available. As mentioned in the earlier section on "Life Cycles", adult sockeye, a few weeks prior to heading to their home streams to spawn are said to gorge on any convenient feed to supplement needed protein.

Although you couldn't prove it by me at that time, the most important piece of information was that description of possible feed deviation as adults. I wasn't particularly interested in juveniles, but the question remained how would I locate adult schools? A fisheries biologist helped me by mapping known return migration routes down through Vancouver Island waters. Runs headed for Homathko, Squamish and Fraser Rivers funneled through Johnstone Strait, normally in July and August. My biologist friend also gave me some tips on the type of water they were likely to be in and probable feed they would be after—though he didn't want to be "quoted" because it is not generally accepted that sockeye switch to vertebrate feed. He believes it though, because sockeye caught commercially sometimes have the evidence in their stomachs.

I modified some coho patterns into smaller versions of Firecrackers, Polar Herring and Polar Shrimp, and tied a dozen very small very sparse fluorescent-pink, red, and lime green shrimp patterns in single colors on size 10 hooks. I reasoned long, fairly light leaders would be required with the small flies, and no more than a 6-weight to 8-weight rod. Rods are so personal. Sockeye aren't big, six to eight pounds, but pound for pound I believe they are the hardest fighting of all salmon, and I had to keep in mind that on several occasions I'd hooked springs over 20 pounds while fishing for smaller species. Anything less than a 6-weight rod would be a stretch. It was also important to have a rod and terminal gear heavy enough to land fish before they fought beyond the recovery stage.

Lines were also a serious consideration. Much of my time would be spent fishing in tide rips. They can be awesome in the water I planned to be in.

Roaring and churning like mid-ocean rivers, rips literally tear baitfish from the safety of kelp and deep holes and bring deep-dwelling crustaceans and planktons boiling to the surface, providing a smorgasbord for salmon and other predators strong enough to withstand the surge. Lines would be shooting tapers in extra-fast sink rates. My rods would handle 300 to 330 grain 30-foot commercial tapers but I wanted short ones which are easier in fast-moving water, so I cut strips of 36-pound-test lead-core. I also had one each 450-grain and 550-grain extra-fast sink tapers that I rarely used because they were so hard to cast, so I cut off ten feet of the slender end to make casting easier (now I buy 550-, 700-, and even 850-grain tapers and routinely cut off the back ten or 12-feet...much easier to use this way). A WF8 floating taper rounded out my lines.

Of course, as mentioned, a quality saltwater fly reel capable of holding 200 or more yards of 25- to 30-pound-test backing is essential. I have two models that I use for the majority of my salmon fishing: Pflueger Supreme model 578 (mentioned often throughout the book), and a No. 4 Fin-Nor. I also have a couple of back-up reels including a Diawa 175 light "mooching" reel. This last one isn't a true fly reel, but it is inexpensive, single-action, has an adequate drag and holds the amount of backing I require (in truth it's rare to have over 100-yards of line pulled off a reel, but I have been spooled more than once by a big spring. You can also chase them with the boat, but a hot fish can take out 200-yards of line in a hurry so I always like to have the insurance).

On August 20 (my birthday if you want to send me a present) I set up in a "deserted" Bauza Cove Camp. Word from the water was that only a very few pinks were left and no one had hit coho or springs—other than the odd straggler—in over ten days. The runs of summer were considered finished here, but a few die-hards were still around. An hour before afternoon flood tide I was on the water, looking.

Two miles out I found the first good rip starting to develop inside the west end of Hanson Island. Gulls and terns were hovering over the water, screeching and dipping down to grab baitfish pushed up by diving sea-pigeons. As I coasted quietly in I could also see fish boiling on the herring school. Quickly matching bait size I tied a three inch long Firecracker to 10-pound-test leader tippet using a loop knot (so the fly would move more freely), and fired into the school. I let the fly sink about ten feet then stripped once. A solid strike came back up the rod and a pink somersaulted over my line and threw the hook. "Oh wonderful...pinks." Then I could see them, zipping under me, beady little eyes glowing. Before I could retrieve my line I had another one on, twisting and spinning like a wind chime. Out of this place! I didn't need confidence-builders—yet. I carefully released the pink, powered up and went hunting.

Out beyond Stubbs' Island, a rock thumb that sticks up between Donegal Head and Hanson Island, I could see another rip beginning to roll. No birds, but that didn't mean no fish. Stopping at the forward crest of waves I cast long and let the rip have its way with my line. I waited a full minute before starting a slow erratic retrieve. I honestly expected a strike, but when it came I wasn't ready for so much power. The fish absolutely pounded my fly, then ripped across the surface like a hydroplane. In retrospect I believe it had already hooked itself while my line was slack, panicked, and hit the end going full bore. What a great fish. Surging runs, jumps, head shakes. Twice I had it to the boat but lost pressure and had to repeat the act. Finally I leaned over and got my hand under it, a gasping ten or 12 pound coho. I wanted sockeye, but not badly enough to give up this kind of sport. I released it and spent the rest of the evening following the rip and casting to slashing fish. By dark I had landed four and lost several more than that. Yeah, fish sure were scarce this year...

In camp I renewed acquaintance with several old fly fishers I recognized from previous trips. Over a splash of single malt we talked about hot spots. The coho I had taken were part of the first good run in two weeks. A few resident springs were in the giant gyre at the east tip of Hanson where waters from Blackfish Sound poured through to meet Johnstone a few miles down, and the last run of pinks were still hanging around in deep water out front. Chums hadn't made their appearance in any quantity as yet.

"What I'm really after are sockeye." I threw it out and let my words lay there. Another splash of Glenfiddich went around and finally it came out that they had been fishing a big school of sockeye right in the monstrous killer rip at the head of Johnstone Strait.

"Can't get the bloody beggars on flies to save my life," offered old Dave, "but Daniel here, he's taken a couple. I been using this half-ounce silver Zzinger with a single hook and doing all right...but it ain't a fly."

"Right *in* the rip?" I shuddered. I had once lost concentration while fishing there and let my Whaler get caught from behind by a three- or four-foot standing wave. It sucked us in and in seconds a foot of water surged from stern to bow. With any other craft I'm positive we would have capsized. Guys that fish in rips always keep motors running, and fortunately my motor wasn't submerged long enough to put the fire out. I was able to gear forward and carefully steer into calmer water where my bilge pump took over. All three of us had on float-coats, but that didn't make us feel any more confident. It was an extremely exhilarating encounter. I hadn't fished the big rip since.

"Right in the rip..." I sat next to that roaring torrent early the next morning, watching logs and splintered boards, massive tangles of kelp, and tons of indeterminate trash boil to the surface then disappear down deep sucking tide swirls like some hideous, seething cauldron, only to be ejected again further along. I was not in my right mind. I wanted sockeye, and "they" said this is where they were (although "they" weren't out here yet this morning). I eased my boat into the rush and motored towards clean water at the leading tip. "I shouldn't be doing this alone," squeaked a strange voice.

Tide rips are not always dangerous, but you must be constantly aware of changing conditions: a sudden vortex that can suck you down, bulges that lift your boat and slide it to one side, standing waves that suddenly break and fill your boat, debris around your motor. One especially bad time can develop during a storm or wind when waves conceal the danger of a big rip and you don't even realize you're in it until water towers over your boat and comes at you from all directions. I'm gutsy—some say I have a death-wish—but I don't like to mess with Mother ocean. I *have* been on the edge of disaster more times than is rational, but I'm also still around. On this excursion bad things didn't happen, and fishing was sensational.

Once I had overcome my fear of the rip I settled down and worked the water as I had been told: "Find the leading edge. That's where the bait will be." Herring were rolling by as if in a giant revolving fishbowl...suddenly there and just as suddenly swept away. There were also salmon. I could see them ten- or 15- feet below, sliding by. "Casts" were merely 30- or 40-foot side-arm lobs. I had shortened my leader because of the current, and tried to stay connected—as much as possible—in a straight line to my fly. Takes were sometimes soft as a puff, and sometimes savage, and for two hours I was in delirium. I offered every pattern I had—Firecrackers, tiny Polar Herring, the special shrimp patterns, even a sand lance—and I hooked fish on those—but by far the best "pattern" was a wisp of bright pink Hoochy with no more than three or four strands or tentacles. I didn't land every fish, but I did fool them, and that's what I intended. When my boat would drift back too far into the rip I only caught trash. I needed to be at the tip, in clean water and over bait. The "retrieve"—wasn't. Just stay tight to the fly and the tide flow does the rest.

Later I sat in calmer water under a warm August sun and contemplated what I had accomplished. Sockeye on a cast fly in saltwater. Had it been done before? Surely. Could I do it again? Perhaps. Subsequent consensus was this run might have been unique since few fly fishers there had ever consistently caught sockeye in the sea. In rivers, yes, especially in places like Alaska's Kenai River below Skilak Lake, and in estuaries like Alberni Inlet in BC and the outlet below Lake Washington in that state. But not very often out in the ocean. A fluke of nature might have caused these particular fish to rely more on baitfish than on traditional forage. It could also be an annual affair that we are just now beginning to understand. They are rarely taken with conventional salmon gear, yet sports trollers in Alberni Inlet near the town of Port Alberni take fish from the Somass River run on tiny pink Hoochies with every other arm pinched off or inch-long spoons trailed behind flashers. Not great sport, but they do have the secret.

I stayed for three more days and fished the big rip morning and evening until the fish moved south down the Island towards home rivers. I landed more than 20...always when the tide ran and only when I found bait. Sometimes it was shrimp sucked from their deep holds, or needlefish, but usually it was herring. I saw surface-feeders a couple of times in the dawning hours, and always stopped to cast. I suspect they are juveniles—next year's adults, but I don't really know. I never landed one.

Whether next summer will be good for sockeye is anyone's guess. There are a lot of variables. Planning a year away will give you whatever edge is available. Do some research and find travel routes. Fisheries people can help with that. Then find moving tide rips or tide lines that have baitfish—not difficult along the west coast—and see what happens. The "worst" scenario might be that instead of sockeye you'll find the rip full of coho or Chinook.

THE TROUBLE CHINOOK CAN GET YOU INTO

Northern Vancouver Island has not gained fame as a prime Chinook fishery, probably because of weather concerns or because there haven't been enough outsiders there yet to "talk it up." Local fishermen know differently, and I sure have caught them throughout that area, but there are places with "kinder" waters we'll be going to. Nevertheless, it wouldn't be fair to just pass this over.

From Port McNeill it is about 20 miles across Queen Charlotte Strait to Knight Inlet and a bit further along is Kingcome Inlet. Both have historical runs (limited now) of big 40 to 60 pound spring salmon in June and July that attract a lot of attention. It can be a brutal trip across there so I don't recommend it for any but very seaworthy boats. Absolutely no roads exist along that side of the British Columbia mainland and no accommodations other than a few exclusive fly-in fishing camps.

North of Port Hardy (25 miles up BC Hiway 19 from Port McNeill), about 75 ocean miles across Queen Charlotte Sound and just inland from the south tip of Calvert Island, is world-famous Rivers Inlet. Still a pretty decent place to catch Chinooks, but a bit uncomfortable for fly fishing. It has deep fjords with sometimes brutal tides and nasty weather. Record-size springs are taken here each year though chances are only fair that a fly-caught spring could be among them. I have been there on two occasions, and while I did cast flies, the only springs I took were on mooching gear fished deep. I'm sure it can be done with fly gear, but it's just not my type of fishing area.

I mention these places not to tantalize but to set the scene. There are Chinooks in northern waters off Vancouver Island, and big ones. Catching them there the way I like to fish is not that easy. However, memorable trips are not always established by how many fish you land, or how big, or even if you hook any. Sometimes you measure success by how well you fail.

I like to fish alone. My temperament (OK, ego) is such that I find it easier to answer to myself than to others. Some of the guys I fish with are the same way and although we generally get along well when fishing together, there are times when separate agendas dictate doing things independently. My boat is a 17-foot Boston Whaler Montauk equipped with an OMC 100 hp GT high performance outboard, all the recommended electronic gear, dual batteries, emergency rations, extra parts, tools, and 47 gallon fuel capacity. This outfit is fairly easy for one guy to handle, and light enough to launch under wicked circumstances. Alone I can hit a top speed of 42 to 45 mph and cover miles of water cruising at 25 to 30. But even with this extravagant arrangement I sometimes get myself into trouble. Like the day I decided to explore the far side of Queen Charlotte Strait by myself.

The previous two days had been calm and hot and the few Chinooks being caught were taken before sun-up. I started before daylight using the memory in my Loran unit to backtrack through various rock piles and islands and charted a course for the north entrance to Tribune Channel just past Kingcome Inlet. Halfway across the Strait in the early dawn light I saw some diving birds just above a small double island and veered over. My sounder showed baitfish and some larger fish about 20-feet below and because the locale was isolated I felt the big ones were probably springs. Shutting off my engine I was quickly mesmerized by the quiet. Nothing but the soft wash of my boat against the sea and the muted hoots and whistles of awakening bird-life. Lead-core broke the tranquillity. A quick retrieve woke somebody up and it flashed by my boat. My second cast had the same result, but this time it was clearly a big Chinook that charged my fly and turned off at the last instant. I was pumped. A quick flip in the direction it had gone, five seconds to sink, then slow one-foot strips.

The strike was vicious, not like a spring. My 9-foot 12-weight rod smacked down on the water and before I could release the running line my middle finger was streaming blood. Almost in the same motion the fish ripped through the surface clearing the water by five feet. An immense Chinook, probably 35 pounds, crashed down and streaked away as I lifted my rod high to clear line from the floor. I hung on with both hands. About 75- or 80-yards out it stopped and rattled my rod with head shakes. I tested it and it resisted by swimming against the pressure in a wide arc. It was wait-and-see time.

My senses told me something was terribly wrong. You know how you get that queasy rush...? I was concentrating so hard on the salmon I didn't notice the current pulling me towards the narrow slot separating the two small islands. By the time my mind registered, a chute of compressed water swung the boat forward and accelerated it through the opening. I heard a helpless, "Oh, s--t" as the whole works was deposited with a skidding, sickening crunch about half-way across a room-sized flat rock...on a falling tide. Loaded, my outfit probably weighs 2,400 pounds and it was sitting in less than four inches of water. Get the picture? It was leaning crazily to one side as I crawled out to do damage survey. No holes, but a badly chipped center-keel, a bent transducer bracket, and the skeg on my motor was scarred but not broken. The shaft housing was stubbed solidly against the side of the rock so I punched "up" on my hydraulic switch to relieve the pressure and the boat settled a few inches onto my own little island.

I couldn't believe it. There I was hanging on to what was probably the biggest "clean" spring salmon I had ever hooked and stranded on a wet rock with no hope of getting off until the next high tide—at least six hours away—and not sure it would even rise high enough to free me. The next high after that would be over twelve hours away, at about two a.m. Break out the dark glasses, set up a beach chair, have a beer. Fight the fish! Unbelievably it was still hooked. Nearly all 300-yards of backing was out and the line was at a bad angle across a pile of rocks on the corner of one of the two mini-islands. I lifted my rod as high as I could, applied pressure and started reeling. There was heavy resistance but I didn't stop. Several minutes later bright orange running line started filling the spool, and I got *that* feeling.

My big salmon was tired as I lead it towards my rock. Deep water on both sides prevented it from grounding and breaking off. It streaked through the chute, flashed by me and went out the other way. It was huge, bigger than the 35 pounds I had first estimated. Fifty feet away it rolled on the surface. What happened next was absolutely astounding. There was an explosion of water around the salmon and line peeled out with a screech my reel had never made before. The power of the run was scary and it kept going for several seconds Then it stopped. A head popped up about 200-feet away and my salmon was tossed high into the air. Mr. Stellar Sea Lion was having break-fast. I watched the play as I reeled in slack line. I was sick. And I didn't even think to shoot a picture (or the flippered quadraped that stole my fish).

I could spend another two or three pages telling how I fished from my rock for the next *seven* hours and caught a few bottomfish and a 12 pound lingcod that grabbed one of them and wouldn't let go until I smacked it several times with my rod. Even had a dogfish hooked for a short time. Drank all my water and ate my meager lunch. Wiped down my boat and waved to a timber company helicopter. Practiced long shooting taper casts (a guy always needs to do that). Slept for an hour. Checked my hull about a dozen times to make certain it hadn't fractured.

The short version is, the water did rise and I did float. I didn't go on to Kingcome Inlet, but I did stop at Malcolm Island on the way back and cast into a good rip. Caught a pink! And sulked. Chinooks *can* get you into trouble.

MORE CHINOOK

One other area often good for Chinooks is narrow, rock-studded Baronet Passage that runs between the north side of Cracroft Island and Harbledown and Turnour Islands. It branches off Johnstone Strait and courses directly to Knight Inlet, one of several famous Chinook fishing areas. Heavy tidal surges flow through the channel and springs travel this route heading towards Knight in early summer. Ten miles up is a scour-hole 50 to 60 fathoms deep (300 feet to 360 feet), and off to one side is a bay loaded with kelp that usually holds herring or other salmon food.

Twice I have been there when Chinooks moved from the hole up onto the shelf to feed and although I didn't hook any, they sure weren't afraid to follow my flies right to the boat. I believe there is good potential all around the north end of Baronet. There are sometimes strong runs of coho there as well.

Another spot worth trying is about ten miles down from Bauza Cove at Robson Bight. Within yards of the river delta water is more than 150 fathoms deep. Fishing along the edge of this drop-off has produced some monster springs for trollers over the years, but it is "heavy duty" water for fly fishers. Coho and pink salmon move into the estuary fairly often and are much easier, and there is always the possibility that a spring or two will feed there as well.

I fished the point about a mile above the bay in July 1991 and lost a very large Chinook while deep-dredging in 60 feet of water. I never saw it, but it had all the classic spring moves. Long powerful runs, sulking, head shakes. Finally it just came undone. A dozen casts later I hooked another fish. This one stayed deep under my boat and it was a pump-lift-reel program. After a few minutes I realized it was a big bottomfish and ten minutes later a toothy 40ish pound ling smiled at me, thrashed once and snapped my 20-pound tippet. Why it ever took a four inch long Polar Shrimp fly I'll never know...they like big meaty meals.

As stated earlier, Chinook fishing is all right here, but not *great* like at Haida Gwaii, or Kyuquot or Ucluelet on the west coast of Vancouver Island where we'll also visit. You have to work hard under often difficult conditions that may or may not produce. But if you go there for sockeye or coho or pinks bring a rod for springs. There are always a few around.

ALWAYS RELIABLE COHO

Compared to the Port Hardy region just north of here and a few places along the outside of Vancouver Island, the Bauza Cove area doesn't seem to have high concentrations of resident coho. By the time schools reach here they are on their way down Johnstone Strait heading towards inland Vancouver Island waters and they often disappear after only a few days stay. However, there are times when coho are everywhere...and if you hit it during one of those periods the fishing can be memorable.

One area always worth trying is Double Bay, on the Blackfish Sound side of Hanson Island. Trollers parade back and forth across the wide entrance and it doesn't take long to determine when fish are around. As mentioned elsewhere, coho have very aggressive feeding habits and you can almost count on them to eat every couple of hours throughout the day when baitfish are present.

One year in the middle of a heavy three-day gale that restricted everyone to camp, I got tired of tying flies, drinking beer, lying, and playing with kids and decided to risk going out. Waves across Johnstone Strait were real attention-getters, some up to six and eight feet high and miles of white-caps. I rode the troughs across, turned with the wind and stayed close to shore down and around the bottom of Hanson, then up Blackfish Sound to Double Bay where the wind wasn't too bad. Big swells rolled in from Queen Charlotte Strait, but I could handle that.

Inside the smallest of the two bays was a solid mass of three-inch needle-fish, condensed there by wind and tide, and being pounded by coho. Like wolves they would surround a section of the school and stalk back and forth. Then, as if on signal, two or three would slash through the ball at Mach 10 causing a shower of fish at the surface. All the salmon would then go into the maze picking off the stunned and wounded.

I uncased my 6-weight Loomis, snapped on a pearlescent Firecracker trimmed in light green Krystal Flash and repositioned my boat so the wind gusts would drift me across the bay. I was using a Marryat MR 8.5A reel (supposed to be OK to use in salt, but it did corrode a little) with a 270-grain piece of lead-core which I lobbed out and fed some line after. I didn't want to risk trying to cast in the swirling wind. My boat was moving at a good clip so I hardly had to retrieve (yeah...trolling). Within 100-feet I hooked a three or four pound coho that jumped ten times (!), a real free-spirit. Good little fish.

After each drift I would power back to the top of the bay, watch for show-ers of needlefish, putt over and float across the spot. It was great action. On one drift I got a ripping strike and the fish jumped immediately, the biggest coho of the day. It went ballistic, catapulting across the water, diving deep, shaking and vibrating for a good five minutes. At the boat I saw it was hooked deeply in the eye and bleeding badly. I brought it in and quickly killed it. A prime 9 pound male. Sadly, it happens once in awhile that fish get hooked in a mortal place like a gill or the eye, and if they are bleeding heavily you have no choice but to kill them. Several times I have hooked fish in the mouth (saw them take or viewed the position of the fly when they came near the boat), only to have them throw the hook during the action and rehook them-selves in some other place, often somewhere on their body.

Hooks with wide gaps—open hooks—can do a lot of damage. I like to use small hooks for salmon, not larger than size 2 or 1/0 and usually sizes 4 or 6, often on a 2X-long extra-stout shank. I also have a problem using barb-less hooks for salmon (small barbless hooks for trout are fine). I believe hooks as large as the ones I use in saltwater penetrate deeper than barbed hooks and can potentially cause more damage. They also account for more rehooks—at least in my experience—during wild action. But I've also seen some pretty fierce lip and cheek ripping with barbed hooks, so it's probably a tradeoff. I use both under different circumstances. Coho and especially Chinook have tough mouths and small sharp hooks seem to penetrate and hold far better than larger ones.

Short small-hook story: Sometime in the late 1970s after I finally learned how to cast heavy shooting tapers without injuring myself and had landed a few sailfish and large toothy ocean critters on flies, I ordered some special tube-flies for billfish from a fellow in Santa Clara, California. These were *the* hot flies at that time. When the beautifully tied seven to nine inch creations arrived instructions said to use a 7/0 hook (7/0!) and open it to a 9/0. Wow! Well, I followed the instructions, tied up three with the big hooks on 30-pound monofilament (also as directed), and that November I was back in Baja ready to get 'em.

The short version of this is five sails took the flies with big hooks and try as I might, I only hooked one of them and that was on its tongue. I was later told I should have been line-striking because my rod was probably too whimpy to drive in the hook, and in retrospect I'm sure that's what happened. But when I tied on two straight-eyed short shank size 2/0 hooks back to back, I hooked 13 sails and landed 10 of them! One fish was even hooked in the bill and the hook had drilled in past the barb. Short, strong, sharp hooks work. I've proven that to myself and others many times.

I headed back to Bauza after four hours of almost non-stop coho action in Double Bay. The wind had increased down the Strait and crossing was a bit frightening but uneventful. Didn't take on a drop of water which further validated my opinion of Whalers in any water situation. Excellent boats. I thank the company and my children thank them. Linda...I don't know. She thinks my boat is my second wife.

Late the next afternoon the wind flattened and I took a couple of old guys over to Double Bay to show them Valhalla. They only had a little 14-foot car topper and were a bit ocean shy, which is smart in these waters. But the needlefish were gone, along with the coho, and two more hours of scouting only turned up a half dozen stragglers. I rigged two of my 11-foot mooching rods with flies and let the two seasoned trollers hang on to them as we slowly moved around. They were delighted with every strike and had a great time. And what supreme stories they related that night around the campfire "The way it used to be up here..."

SEA RATS AND MYSTERY CHUMS

Good schools of these fish come down Queen Charlotte Strait through Johnstone Strait, pinks from early July through mid-August, and chums a bit later. The biggest overlap of all species is in early August when "anything" might be caught. I've insinuated disregard for pinks several times so far, but that's not really fair. They are honestly fun to catch if you're not preoccupied with hunting more macho species, and if there are no other fish around they can save a trip. Inland waters around Vancouver Island can be loaded with pinks every summer, and in the Courtenay to Campbell River area they can be caught from shore along estuaries into September. They are incredibly abundant, not commercially targeted, don't can or freeze well, but are not bad eating fresh. Sautéed or poached in white wine, with mushrooms... Don't hesitate to try a few for camp meals. Many restaurants will prepare your fish if you are motelling it.

As mentioned earlier, chum salmon are anyone's guess. I don't know many guys who can tell you much about chum runs. They are a prolific species and are *great* fighters on fly gear. About all I can say is you might run into them while fishing for coho or Chinook anywhere along the northern part of Vancouver Island or along the BC mainland from the Alaska panhandle down the coast. Other than around the Queen Charlotte Islands where they are caught with fair regularity, they are a true enigma to fishermen everywhere.

PORT HARDY, B.C.

North of Port McNeill about 25 miles is the town Port Hardy, best known among the fishing crowd for great coho fishing. Locals claim if the existing world record coho of 32 pounds is ever broken it will probably come from the waters around here.

With a population of about 6,000, this rough-and-ready town offers its commercial fishing and logging community surprisingly complete amenities, and tourism is increasing every year as outsiders learn about the outstanding saltwater fishing here. There are plenty of camping and RV sites around, but very few other accommodations, so plan accordingly. Dock space is also next to impossible, and rigs with boats that can be launched and hauled out each day will be a great advantage. There are two ramps: A free three lane city ramp at the Quarterdeck Marina that always seems to be crowded and busy, and one at Bear Cove across Hardy Bay. This is the one I use. Not bad. A bit steep, but parking is much easier here. It also puts you a little closer to fishing.

Of all the places I will tell you about, this is one area that can really have ugly weather. Generally the winds of summer aren't too bad, but wind or fog can hit quickly. Like the Port McNeill/Bauza area we just talked about and all along the outside west coast waters, clear days are ones to watch. Fierce winds can develop very suddenly, and if it gets hot inland, the rising heat seems to suck fog right down the channel. Small boats like car toppers are not recommended out past Hardy Bay unless traveling with another boat. And even then, watch the weather. We won't even talk about the winters here...

If you bring your family, there are plenty of bottomfish to keep them busy while you're fly fishing. This is without question one of the best areas for all species of rockfish, halibut and lingcod I've ever seen. Small-craft commercial fishermen are starting to exploit this abundance, but the area is vast and for now at least appears to be holding its own.

CHINOOK

I have only fished Port Hardy waters on two occasions, both times as extensions of trips to Bauza. The first time was in July, too early for big coho but just in time for Chinook. They averaged 20 pounds and acted like coho...right in your face and screamers when hooked. Larger fish do come through but I'm told they tend to stay deep and are better suited to trollers with downriggers. I've never fished for those but I'm positive with a little research it wouldn't take long to find places where they feed or shallow channels they move through, as well as areas where our deep water fly techniques would work.

The only area I tried was out around the Gordon Islands group. Consummate fishing waters these, with superb possibilities. But salmon can also be found close to Hardy off Dillon Point and the islands just out from there as well as inside Hardy Bay. I won't pretend to know much about this area for spring salmon fishing, but it has many of the classic rocky points, kelp beds, inlets and routes that good Chinook water everywhere has, so I suspect wherever bait can be found, deep or at the surface, Chinook will be around.

COHO

Coho start showing up in Hardy around the middle of July and there will be runs right through October. These are big fish, six to eight pounds when they arrive, and some will be upwards of 20 by September. My second and last trip was in August and although big coho were being taken in deep bait schools by sports trollers, I had a tough time because of wind. The best day I had was four fish to 12 pounds on a point of kelp out in the Gordon Islands. Incredible fighting fish.

I hear stories about coho up to 25 pounds being taken here every fall. I have taken several large coho over the years, but none that would approach that. A 21 pounder off the north end of Quadra Island near Campbell River a few years ago gave me all I could handle. My equipment is better today, but coho that size are brutal fighters. I love it.

SOCKEYE, PINK AND CHUM SALMON

There are very reliable sockeye and pink runs here, mainly in July and August. These are the same fish that we intercept in the rips farther down Johnstone Strait, but up here the run is most often out in the Queen Charlotte Strait...which is a pretty fair distance, although some years they have been right outside the Port Hardy harbor. Chums show up later in August and as in other areas, not many fishermen specifically target them.

So it's all here. Given more time to explore I'm positive it will prove to be as good as or better than the area down around Port McNeill. At this stage Hardy is really untapped by recreational fishermen and I'm just not familiar enough with the spots to make specific recommendations. I can tell you to go here with every confidence, however, and do some exploring...especially in late July and early August.

GETTING THERE

Crossing the border into Canada is easy for American citizens. Just carry valid ID and make sure your vehicles and trailers are insured in your own home state. At the I-5 Canada/US border crossing from Washington state into British Columbia, I-5 turns into BC Provincial Highway 99. Drive about 25-miles and take BC Provincial Highway 17 west to BC Ferry terminal at Tsawwassen (pronounced too-wah-sun). It's well marked. Pay your tuition and drive onto either the ferry going to Victoria or Nanaimo on Vancouver Island. If you haven't traveled on the BC Ferry system, it's a treat! They're fast and efficient, and can take any rig you can drive or haul. If you are in a position to take a motor home and tow a good ocean boat, by all means do it. It's expensive but the accommodations will be more dependable and the launch ramps in Bauza Cove, Port McNeill and Port Hardy—and other places along the way—can easily handle it.

You can also ferry across from Port Angeles, Washington to downtown Victoria, but be careful just showing up and expecting to get on-board. That ferry is almost always full in summer, and can't handle larger sized vehicles *as efficiently* as BC ferries. Call ahead...but I believe it's a first-come-first-served kind of deal.

If you bring family (or a spouse who isn't used to being left alone while you're out doing your thing), I recommend starting out or ending your trip in Victoria so they will have something positive (or romantic) to remember from the trip. I will catch hell from the resort people in Port McNeill and Port Hardy areas for saying that, but truthfully, unless your family enjoys boating and fishing with you, there is little else for them to do in the northern part of the Island. Kids are kids anywhere, and they find things to do in the creeks and in camp or along the shore, but it is confining and sometimes wet up there, and there are more than a few mosquitoes and no-see-ums (voracious little bastards, these), so rubber boots and long sleeves are recommended.

There *is* one adventure the whole family would enjoy while in the north and that is an excursion to whale-watch. There are several pods of killer whales that live around Blackfish Sound and an old ship takes tours a couple of times daily right from Bauza Cove. I've been on it and it is fun. I have also been approached to within 20-feet by a pod of killer whales while I was in my own boat, and a little twist to the seafarer's prayer, "Oh Lord, thy fish are (sea is) so big and my boat is so small..." becomes very meaningful at a time like that. There are federal regulations about staying a certain distance away from whales—I believe it's 100-yards—but I didn't have a choice in this instance.

There is also a BC Ferry terminal in Horseshoe Bay, north of Vancouver BC on Transcanada 1, with ferries that go directly to Nanaimo. Leave Nanaimo and drive north to Campbell River on BC Provincial 19. It is nearly all two-lane and can be very slow with summer traffic, but there are numerous towns, motels, resorts, launches, stores, restaurants, fuel, etc., along the way to Campbell River. To get to our fishing destinations stay on BC 19 . The traffic won't be too bad after you leave Campbell River, and after Sayward—about 40 miles—the hiway becomes one of the best in the province.

From Campbell River it's about 145 miles to Port Hardy and there are almost no services along the way until you reach Port McNeill. Much of northern Vancouver Island is undeveloped for tourism except right in those two towns. Take all the fly tackle and equipment you think you will need. Fishing resorts and camps have lots of trolling and terminal gear—line, hooks, lures—but almost no fly gear. There are some exceptions, a few sporting goods stores along the way (i.e., Campbell River) do stock some saltwater fly patterns, tying materials, hooks, etc., but don't count on much. In a pinch you could buy bucktails and use those. Fuel, groceries, clothing, and other such essentials are readily available.

Bauza Cove Camp is reached off of Highway 19 via Beaver Cove/Telegraph Cove Road about five miles before you reach Port McNeill, and there is another campground at Alder Bay just west of Telegraph Cove down the same road. Both have launch ramps and full hookup RV sites...and are often fully booked from mid-June through early August, so call ahead to reserve a camp space and boat slip. There are also a few motels in Port McNeill and Port Hardy, but as mentioned in the text rooms are usually booked, so again, call ahead.

Boats are available for rent at some docks on a limited basis, but *please*, if you take your own make certain it is seaworthy. And take plenty of clothes for all weather conditions (this includes every area we talk about). I've been there when it was 80 degrees in May and 40 degrees in mid-August. Normally those temps are the other way around, but even when it's nice on land fog and mist can make boating a chilly experience.

Boaters should obtain marine nautical charts 3546, 3548 and 3549 for Port McNeill and Port Hardy areas. Order a catalog of Pacific Coast Nautical Charts from Canadian Hydrographic Service, Department of Fisheries and Oceans, P.O. Box 6000, Sidney, B.C. V8L 4B2. This will list charts you can purchase for every area along the Pacific west coast.

Again, I also suggest you write: Ministry of Tourism, Parliament Buildings, Victoria, B.C. V8V 1X4, and ask for a British Columbia road map, an Accommodation and Travel Guide, and a Campground Directory for more specific information on where to stay. Additional information can also be obtained from Port McNeill Travel Infocentre, P.O. Box 129, Port McNeill, B.C. V0N 2R0. They will have a list of guides as well as accommodations available.

If you are an adventurer and/or a serious saltwater fly fisher...trust me, you'll love it up there.

Robert H. Jones

SALMON TO A FLY

FOUR

Vancouver Island — Inland

Campbell River, B.C.

*I*f fishing success is measured by the highest annual average catch per boat per day then the Campbell River area wins the title hands down. Unquestionably the most famous salmon fishing destination on the west coast, Campbell River has been advertised as "Salmon Capital of the World" for more than a half-century. More remote places like Langara Island in the Queen Charlottes, Rivers Inlet, or Kyuquot on the outside of Vancouver Island may yield larger salmon, but no other destination is so dedicated to angler success. Campbell River "mystique" still draws fishermen.

Ordinarily a book about fly fishing for salmon in the open ocean wouldn't include Campbell River since it is located halfway up the protected inside waters of Vancouver Island. But because this place has been the training ground for at least several dozen would-be saltwater fly fishers—including myself—and has been responsible for opening many eyes to the positive philosophies of fisheries conservation, I feel it is an important place to mention. This is where the wonderful books about rivers and streams and salmonids were written by Roderick Haig-Brown between 1931 and 1974. And it's where much of what we know about fly fishing for Pacific salmon and steelhead originated.

ORIGINAL INHABITANTS

Information obtained from *The Indian History of British Columbia* by Wilson Duff, Provincial Museum of BC; and from *Indian Tribes of the Northwest* by Reg Ashwell, Hancock House Publication.

The original occupants of this region were a tiny, peaceful clan of Coast Salish Indians...the Pentlatch (Courtenay's Puntledge River is apparently named for these, although the spelling took a wrong turn somewhere along the way). The Pentlatch eventually joined with another Coast Salish band, the Island Comox and in a short time their bloodline became extinct. Archaeological evidence from middens ("dumps" of shells, bone and other refuse at various settlements), certain unique layout patterns of aboriginal sites, and other artifacts indicate occupation of the area between Campbell River and Comox for several thousand years.

Like the majority of North Pacific Coast Indian peoples, cultural resources came from the sea and the forest, and this region provided great bounty. Blacktail deer, mountain lion and black bear were—and still are—abundant (although these were not utilized much in diets of coastal Indians). In summer, salmonberries, wild raspberries, and currents were gathered. Rivers and lush estuaries gave them waterfowl, trout and spawning salmon. Tidal points had mussels, beaches and gravel bars produced clams, and edible kelps and seaweed grew everywhere along the shore. Natives were excellent fishermen and in only a few months each summer were able to obtain provisions for the entire year plus have a surplus for trade with other clans. Estimates are that three quarters of their food came from the sea and 75 percent of that was salmon.

Coastal Indian one-piece war canoes and dugouts were legendary. What is not so well known was their use of huge red cedar planks split from standing trees for longhouses and other dwellings, and yellow cedar carved into dishes and eating implements, storage boxes and chests. Even the inner bark of cedars was used—peeled, soaked and pounded into separate fibers which were tightly woven into garments, baskets, blankets and other articles that still amaze today with their durability.

Sometime in the early 1800s the very aggressive Lekwiltok, a Kwakiutlan band from Johnstone Strait area moved south and displaced the Island Comox. Within 100 years their were no "pure" Island Comox left, and remaining natives in the area from present-day Campbell River to Courtenay-Comox were themselves displaced by a strong population of white settlers.

FOUNDATION

This history is for me a bit of nostalgia. My own family roots go back to 1870 in the Comox Valley where a distant relative—I believe it was a brother of my father's grandfather—came to farm. Stories were handed down about the extraordinary runs of salmon in every stream and river, and about natives of that time. In 1956 my dad and I made a pilgrimage-of-sorts from our home at Lake Tahoe to Vancouver Island and Comox and Campbell River to see the source for these stories. We met two families related to us which, I am ashamed to admit, we immediately lost touch with, but both corroborated many of the family chronicles. We also learned that original white settlers probably had little time to fish but rather bartered farm goods for fish or bought from natives. Our inquiries explained, perhaps, why I am so drawn to this island and this place...but from where, I wondered, had I earned my lifelong fanaticism for fishing? Someday maybe I'll take on the family genealogy and do it right.

In 1970, a century after my ancestors settled here, I made my own journey to Campbell River and met Walter Crawford who owned Bennett's Point Resort, a fishing camp near the Oyster River. We decided we probably weren't related, though I can't remember why, but because of my interest in fly fishing Walt introduced me to his friend Roderick Haig-Brown. I hadn't known anything about this very special person before my visit, but after spending an hour with him in his home overlooking the Campbell River, I came away knowing I had met a wise and dignified and gracious man. Of Haig-Brown's 25 published books I now own several. They are a never-ending source of inspirational philosophy, information, history and immense pleasure.

My passion for fly fishing and knowledge of the salmonid fishery and its synergy with moving waters was and remains puerile compared to Haig-Brown's. His lifelong conviction was to protect British Columbia's rivers from being dammed or ruined by logging, pulp mills and mining, or manufacturing and domestic pollution. Always positive about the future, he wrote and lectured that it was never too late to clean up what had gone askew or to conserve what was still wild. Roderick Haig-Brown died in 1974 and the resources in British Columbia and elsewhere in the west have steadily deteriorated since.

That all-too-brief meeting and reading his thoughtful, passionate philosophy that "The resource is the sacred trust and first responsibility of every angler to ensure its protection and perpetuation" gradually changed my thinking. Years later when I moved to Vancouver Island, I was primed to do my part to preserve the value of it all. Sadly I have so far failed miserably. Too caught up with the day to day mechanics of getting along. Agreeing sometimes when I shouldn't. Allowing myself to be persuaded when my own stand would have been more meaningful. Not taking a stand at all. Taking the wrong stand.

There are many ways to fish and we all know them—perhaps have taken part in and enjoyed more than one—trolling, jigging, spin casting, bait fishing, fly fishing.Each has its own special following and appeal. Yet I tend to feel superior when I am casting a fly over slashing salmon and someone trolls by and I choose not to remember that at one stage in my advancement towards my presently preferred method of fishing I too enjoyed trolling or bucktailing. Wrong stand! It doesn't matter how I feel about it. Fishing in itself is an insignificant part of the act of enjoying fish. The most important component is realizing that without the resource the pleasure of fishing, or the enjoyment of seeing fish, or just knowing they are there, could not exist.

It is important for all fishermen to understand this and feel it whenever they are on the water. It is our duty to be conservators every time we engage this resource in any manner, and to speak out whenever we see it being threatened (I prefer *con*servator which in my terminology refers to proper use and respect of resources rather than *pre*servator which alludes to not using resources at all, but rather, just leaving them alone).

It has taken me many years to compose my current philosophy about standing up for resources and environment. Emotions are pounded so hard by seeing the torment caused to the land, forests, rivers, fish and other wild critters that eventually you can't help but react. At first I ran around in circles until I fell down, exhausted and discouraged because I couldn't do anything meaningful to save the planet. It was like the 60s all over again (yes, I *was* part of that era albeit at a distance). Gradually I became aware of the real problems and was able to focus on specific issues. Now I feel capable of taking a stand for what I believe is right. I no longer seek direction or approval or permission. The space I take up now has become purposeful and I will pursue in particular the fisheries resource in a way that makes me feel good.

CHASING COHO

I hooked my first-ever Pacific salmon—a Chinook—on a cast fly in the waters of Washington state, but I gained proficiency in Campbell River fishing for "bluebacks," immature coho up to about two pounds. These feisty little guys are easy to catch, but sometimes can be extremely selective. Cast thousands of times to them over a 25-year period and you can't help but learn a few things.

Early in the summer bluebacks show up across Discovery Passage on the south end of Quadra Island. A large shallow bank—Wilby Shoal—begins just south of Cape Mudge Lighthouse and stretches east to Francisco Point. Loaded with kelp beds, big rocks, gravel and sand flats, and protected from prevailing summer winds, it's a giant holding tank for baitfish and an outstanding classroom for fly fishers. When salmon are abundant, anyone and everyone catches them. When they're scarce, experience is the key to success.

At first bluebacks stay near the surface feeding on krill and planktons. Dimpling fish can be caught on the same sparsely-dressed pink or red flies that we use for sockeye. Action can be fast and furious, and while I usually don't relate this figure, a friend and I once had a 100+ day using size 10 pink pearlessence Mylar flies. It was a slaughter, and attests to the aggressive behavior of coho. Cast to them and they will come.

As summer progresses, and depending on availability of feed, coho will stay around the banks and continue to grow. Baitfish grow larger as well, and when bluebacks switch over to baitfish, some serious fish-catching begins. I have been on Wilby Shoal probably every day of July and August over the years, and a few times in May, June, September and October. I won't even try to estimate the numbers of fish I have blundered into here during the 25 or so years I have fished it. It is *still* one of the most productive areas on Vancouver Island.

Flies of late summer *must* match bait size and color or they won't generate much interest. Herring and needlefish will be the predominant feed, and if there is a lot of it around, coho will be quite selective. Herring in this water usually have bright blue-green backs, silver sides and white bellies. Patterns tied with bright-white polar bear hair (sometimes available from taxidermists), white bucktail, goat hair, synthetic "hair," or Mylar tubing with Krystal Flash or Flashabou to match back colors will take fish. Some years I have seen herring with cobalt-blue and even olive-gray backs, so pay particular attention to color. My Firecrackers all have a few strands of Krystal Flash added to give them the right flash of color.

Sand lance (called needlefish in BC) are usually light- or pale-green on the back, and sometimes olive-brown, with white bellies. My opinion is if good quantities of herring are present salmon tend to ignore needlefish, but you should always have a few patterns.

One hot day in August I was having a heck of a time taking coho. None of my herring patterns worked even though I was finding a few schools of herring and there were salmon around. Once in a while one would take a look, but rarely did they hit. During one fast retrieve I snagged a herring and—after looking around to be certain no one was watching—I left it in the water struggling on the hook. An eight pound Chinook streaked out of nowhere and nailed it right in front of me. I got so excited I snapped the rod up, lost my grip on the fly line and threw half-hitches around everything in sight. Been there, done that before...

After re-tooling, I motored along under the high sand cliffs towards the long rock reef and kelp bed just east of the Discovery rip. On the southern-most point I ran over a big school of needlefish undulating like eels in rhyth-mic cadence with the tidal current. There were no salmon visible, but this was a big school and since I was having *so* much luck using herring pat-terns... What the heck! I tied up to the last kelp bulb in line and drifted back far enough to make casting to the school comfortable.

My original needlefish patterns were stubbornly artistic creations. About three inches of silver Mylar tubing over size 8 4X-long hooks with painted-on white bellies and pale green backs. They didn't twist or roll. The tails just sort of wiggled with the retrieve. I'd never even had a hit on one. OK, I was desperate.

I made several casts without even a follow and was thinking about moving when a shower of baitfish erupted from the edge of the kelp. I was using a full dry line at the time, and I had wrapped about half an inch of lead wire at the head of each hook before tying. With every cast the line would hit the water and then the heavy fly would plunk down somewhere in the same vicinity. With bait jumping everywhere I got in a hurry, dropped my backcast and my fly hit the side of the boat—just as a huge coho slashed across the surface.

Quickly checking the fly I saw the point was broken off. I fumbled another one onto my leader and lobbed it towards the last spot I'd seen the fish. I let it sink for a few seconds and on the first strip I got an absolutely savage strike. My rod bucked for a couple of head shakes, then line peeled off the reel and the fish ripped through the surface, hit the water and went airborne five or six times. It was at least ten pounds. All I could think of was keeping the line clear of kelp, bow line, engine, prop, other boats... Then it went to the bottom and rattled. I could see it about 20-feet below throwing its head. One more good jump—almost into the boat, a short run, then to the net. I remember the entire sequence like it was on video. The coho was completely exhausted when I cradled it to remove my fly. A short rest and it swam strongly away. A fabulous fish.

I caught two more that day on the same fly—though both fish were smaller. I have had only a few occasions to use a needlefish pattern since, though I now tie them Firecracker-style—long, tubular pearl-white with green Krystal Flash back and flowing tails and a slight bend at the head to give them a roll. I also bought a dozen Tabory's Sand Lance patterns from Orvis. You just never know!

NORTHERNS—KINGS OF COHO

One year I pulled off the highway at Willow Point on Labor Day weekend and looked across at Wilby Shoal. It was only 7 a.m. and there had to be 300 boats on the water. "No way we're going to try to fight that crowd," I told my partner. "Let's go on up to Seymour Narrows and put in." The tides weren't too bad that week and I hoped there might be some coho or springs moving down from Johnstone Strait.

Seymour Narrows has some of the most treacherous water around Vancouver Island, worse even than the big rips in Johnstone. Steep rock walls compress the channel to less than a half-mile and when tide flows are heavy the current might hit 15 mph through there. I've been in it. It's like challenging stretches of Class IV and V river rapids—mean waves, wild turbulence capable of picking up a boat and throwing it several feet, extreme cross currents, sucking holes that drop out from under you. "Exhilarating" as my friend Bob Jones likes to say. Right... But there are usually Chinooks here and for those brave enough to challenge, the rewards can be awesome. I wasn't in that frame of mind this day.

We started at the top end of the Narrows at Brown's Bay. There were a few boats off the mouth motor mooching for Chinooks but no one had taken a fish in three hours. It was already 11 a.m. and the sun had burned-off the morning haze. I opted to run across the channel and up around the point to Deepwater Bay. At the top end is an underwater reef that comes up within 60 feet of the surface and inside it is a tidy kelp bed that usually has bait. This area at the top end of Quadra Island takes a heavy flush of water on the flood tide and we would be in place about an hour before high slack.

There was a cold wind moving with the tide and some choppy whitecaps as we crossed Discovery Passage. No boats around Plumper Point, which wasn't unusual with the bite further down the Narrows at Maud Island. No one was in the Bay either. We had it all to ourselves, which might be an indicator of something not so good.

Running across to the rocky shoreline of Quadra I slowed and John rigged his lightweight ten-foot mooching rod and stripped out his favorite polar bear hair bucktail—a red, white and blue Coronation. I moved along the rocks and kelp reefs at "bucktail speed," just fast enough to keep the fly darting along beneath the wake and popping up to skim the surface from time to time.

We were passing a tumble of rocks with sparse kelp when John got a good strike. The rod was in his hands but he missed. I circled and came back across the same spot and this time he nailed a rocket-minded coho that launched as soon as it hit. End over end about three times and the hook came out. "Wow, did you see that?"

"Let's cast. You can strip off enough monofilament to wing it out 40- or 50-feet I'm sure. Strip it fast. Here, let me show you." I took his rod and peeled a bunch of line onto the floor and side-armed the bulky six-inch long fly right into the kelp. The fish he had lost looked about eight or nine pounds.

The tide was really running, pushing us along faster than I wanted. Within seconds the bucktail was being dragged across the surface by the current and as I started a fast strip there was an eruption at the end of my (John's) line.

A huge salmon churned out of the water, took one look at the boat, and headed out towards Seymour Narrows. I forfeited over 100-yards of line on that first run and looking down I discovered there weren't many wraps left on John's little mooching reel. "John, how much line do you have on here?" He couldn't remember if it was 150- or 200-yards. Never had I felt so little control over a situation. "Better fire things up and chase this critter. He's almost got us spooled." I was sure it was a Chinook.

A hundred yards away the fish turned and ran parallel to us—and jumped. Then a short rush and another jump. Again, and then again as we neared it. I had recovered all but about 30-yards and was beginning to feel comfortable when it headed straight for the boat and screamed by just behind us—and jumped again. "John, it's a coho. A monster coho!" My adrenaline surged to an all-time high. I'd never hooked a coho this big on such a flimsy rod.

We played cat and mouse for a bit, then after resting he charged off again, 50-yards and several more spectacular jumps this time. But I knew I had him. Another ten minutes and he was in the net...a great hook-nosed male...a northern! I hooked my scale to the rim of the net and gently hoisted it. Twenty-three pounds. Allowing about two pounds for the net, it was the greatest coho I had (have) ever landed. He charged away as soon as I reversed the net from around him. "Nice fish," remarked John in his usual understated way. Indeed... I've hooked probably a dozen northerns over the years, and landed a couple around 16 or 17 pounds (lost all the bigger ones!), but this one was special because it was the biggest I had ever landed on light weight "traditional" coho gear and a "cast" fly (well, I *did* cast that bucktail).

No one really seems to know if these bigger-than-normal coho salmon are separate species or are just an aberration of nature. I've read stories and talked to people who have pretty strong opinions about origins. Everything from they are born and reared in northern streams and get down into southern waters in their migration patterns, to they are special stocks that live up to five years and get bigger because they spend more time feeding, to they only live the normal three years but are a separate and distinct species. Even fisheries experts differ on why a 25 or 30 pound coho is sometimes caught in a school of predominately six or eight pounders, or why a run of all monster-size coho shows up in an area one year, provides spectacular fishing for a week or two then is never seen again. Was it a quirk of nature that a particular run got more feed, or were procreated by a rare strain of enormous parents (most plausible), or perhaps the fertile eggs were nuked and the offspring mutated into giants?

I sure don't have the answer, but I do know if you can hook one you're in for the thrill of your life! The best time along our coast—from Oregon to northern British Columbia—is from Labor Day through October and even into November. All the places I have talked about so far, Queen Charlotte Islands, Port Hardy and Port McNeill, as well as places coming up in the next section—Kyuquot, Nootka, Clayoquot and Ucluelet all have their share of northern coho, though numbers of large fish caught on sports gear are constantly decreasing (as, in fact, are all coho along the west coast!). Probably Port Hardy and Haida Gwaii are the best spots now. I've rarely had time in the fall to go that far, so I never have, but as I get older I'm told I'll have more time. Hopefully I'll remember what to do with it.

Methods of taking northerns are also unique and those who are purist fly casters won't like what I am about to describe. Northerns like big, fast-moving flies. And I mean *big* and *fast*. Flies four to six inches long would be minimum, tied in baitfish colors—purple and white, blue-green and white, cobalt blue and white, red, white and blue... They're a bugger to cast, but the retrieve is even more difficult. Fast and continuous is the key, and while conventional retrieves sometimes produce (as in my case), they won't consistently do it! The trick is to keep your boat moving as you retrieve your fly!

Boat speed is determined by letting your fly trail behind in the wake for a minute. It should remain just under the surface as the boat moves, and jump out of the water once in awhile when you strip in. The nearest parallel I can think of is casting to the bank while moving down a river in a drift boat and then letting the line slide back behind as you bring it in.

Cast into kelp beds, along reefs and over bait schools as you move and if you don't get a hit let your fly swing back into the wake and trail for a moment or two before stripping in to recast. A plastic baby bathenette Velcroed to the floor of my boat to strip into allows better line control and makes casting easier. And I advise using a full floating WF or saltwater taper fly line rather than a shooting taper for this type of fishing. Full fly lines are much easier to cast and control, and stripping while in a moving boat isn't as deadly on fingers as running lines when you get a strike or a snag.

Keep your rod tip right on the water—even under the surface—and when a fish hits, hand-strike quickly but *don't* hold onto the line with your stripping hand after you do! Just control any line that is on the floor of your boat or in your stripping basket from getting fouled or tangled. You want to play it from the reel so wait until the fish finishes its first run or until the boat has pulled the slack before you set yourself to fight. Of course, stop the boat as soon as you can to prevent too much line from running out.

Unless the motor is shut off when you actually hook the fish this method eliminates any would-be world record, and if that is your goal then use the billfish method of trolling an attractor fly without a hook. Coho will come after it and sometimes follow it right to the boat, giving you an opportunity to stop and cast. But even if they are in a feeding mood, chances are only fair one will hit. Several of us tried this in the early 80s after good success in Mexico on sailfish and marlin using attractors, but we were more often disappointed than successful using it on salmon. Usually what happens is northern coho will follow the cast fly but for some reason won't hit it as readily as if it is trailing in the wake. Old-timers say the bubbles created by the moving boat and propeller look like a school of baitfish and the fly skipping around in it is irresistible to them. Sounds reasonable. All I know is it does work when northerns are around!

One credible theory about why the numbers of salmon being caught is declining is that the schools are staying deeper. The majority of recreational coho fishing is done in the top 40-feet of water, and for northerns—right on the surface. Commercial trollers continue to take Chinook, chum, and coho of all sizes at depths far deeper which virtually eliminates fly fishing.

The reason may be due to recent climatic effects mentioned earlier that changed the surface production of nutrients on which the food chain is dependent. Any interruption of this and baitfish must look elsewhere for their sustenance, either in other regions of the sea or in deeper water where certain other zooplanktons are produced. If upsurges don't carry these to the upper levels, baitfish would have to stay deeper and predator species such as salmon would as well.

Other speculation now in vogue is that coho stocks programmed to use upper levels of water have been depleted and only deep water fish remain. Some federal fisheries personnel truly believe this is the case based on tagging and catch studies, as well as sonar tests that indicate schools may be "learning" to swim deep enough to avoid seine nets.

In either event, it appears we will have to devise new methods of locating and fishing for all species of salmon, including northerns. But believe me, they are well worth the effort!

CHINOOK FOR THE BOOK

I'm sure you have conjectured I'm a bit of a loner. I don't like crowds and the few people who choose to crony with me are more-often-than-not much like me. Not that I'm a recluse or secretive. I'll tell anyone who asks (well, *almost* anyone) what fly I'm using or my methods or what brand(s) of scotch I drink—hell, I'll even share with them if I see the right twinkle in their eye. But there is one group of people I wouldn't mind being associated with: the Tyee Club of British Columbia where membership is based solely on angling performance.

To earn member status and the fabled gold Tyee Club pin an angler must register at the clubhouse on Tyee Spit in Campbell River, pay a $5.00 annual entry fee, and go out onto the waters surrounding the mouth of the Campbell River between July 15 and September 15, and land a Chinook salmon weighing 30 pounds or more while fishing from a rowed boat.

Tackle rules date back to 1924 and are very specific: rods must be between six and nine feet, line must have a breaking point of no more than

20-pounds, and the lure must be artificial with a single hook. Most anglers use plugs or spoons, but flies are also allowed. If a fish that qualifies is caught, line (or leader) testing is done at the clubhouse and if it passes a simple dead-lift test, you earn your membership. Easy, right?

Well, I know three individuals who are *excellent* fishermen and have tried it dozens of times over the last 10 years and still haven't qualified. Rowboats and guides are available from several sources in Campbell River—one has only to ask around—but as can be appreciated, the best guides are usually reserved a year in advance. The first summer I decided to try it I couldn't afford a "real" guide so I talked my father-in-law, Hugh Fletcher, into using his 12-foot aluminum boat and doing the rowing.

We decided since it was my idea I would fish for the first hour, then it would be his turn, then mine and so on (I figured that first hour before sunup would be "our" best opportunity). We had parked our camper at an RV camp on the Spit and were up and out on the water by about 5:30. We motored out to the Tyee Pool on the outside of the Spit and I was surprised to see so many boats there—perhaps 25 or more—including some "sports" trollers who didn't mind making things even more difficult for the rowers. I could see immediately that fly casting was going to be very limited. I wouldn't be able to put out too much line because of boat movement around us, and I'd have to watch my back cast. I decided to just strip cast—peel out 40- or 50-feet of line and lob it out—then let Fletch maneuver the boat while I stayed in touch with things. Fish were rolling in the Pool and one boat had a fish on as we took up a position just at the edge of the strong current. I got ready and as Fletch positioned himself at the oars I shut off the 9.9 and raised it. A quick flip and we were fishing.

My hour went quickly with nothing exciting to report after perhaps a dozen casts. A nice spring was landed near us, too small to qualify. The sun came up over Quadra Island and with it the hustle and bustle of bird life and boat traffic on Discovery Passage. The flotilla from exclusive April Point Lodge headed out for the day, a dozen Boston Whalers each with a guide and two fisher-persons. A few went north, probably to power-mooch fresh herring along Copper Cliffs or at the Dolphins, and the rest aimed south towards Cape Mudge and Wilby Shoal. We heard later that a young newly-wed staying at one of the lodges who had never fished—and hadn't even wanted to—caught her first-ever salmon in the Lighthouse Pool off Mudge that morning—a 52 pound spring. Being the chauvinistic deviate that I am it crossed my mind that her new husband probably choked about that turn of events!

SALMON TO A FLY

As I took my turn at the oars, Fletch put out an old pink and pearl-white plug that someone had given him in his travels. The treble hooks were attached to some sort of sliding nylon line affair and after replacing them with the required single hook we didn't even know how to tie the damn thing onto his line. It had been *years* since I had trolled and even then I'd never used anything like that. But we figured it out. By watching and asking other anglers near us we knew to let out about 20-feet of line then attach a 4 ounce Peetz sliding weight, then let out another 40-feet. In short order I could see the tip of his rod slowly pulsing as I fell into the same rowing rhythm as the other boats and maintained our position. We were truly the ugly duckling amongst the swans in our tin boat. Graceful hand-built wooden dories painted white and edged in natural cedar or oak with bright brass fittings bobbed gently and reacted instantly to any movement of an oar. They skimmed quickly across tidal whirls and over the current while our metal tub did a suction-cup thing. With the current pulling I had to work twice as hard just to keep in place.

A shout of "fish-on" directed our attention for a minute and several boats opened the way for the lucky angler to drift through to open water. When we got back to our program I noticed Fletch's rod had stopped pulsing and was just bending. He was sitting sideways on the seat with his feet up against the gunnel and was right in the middle of a swallow of coffee when the rod lurched and smacked down on the aluminum rim of the stern. Line burned off the reel and a spring about 20 pounds launched out of the water behind us and promptly threw the plug high into the air.

"Fletch, you gotta set the hook with this kind of fishing..." Then I laughed out loud. He had coffee dripping from his glasses and his chin and a long wet stain ran down his front into his crotch. He grinned through the mess. "Man, I don't know what was more exciting...the fish or the hot coffee on old Dooley." We stayed with it for another couple of hours, changing off, and although at least half a dozen springs were landed in other boats, no one entered a Tyee that day.

As we packed up back at the campground we chatted with an old fellow who had been trying to become a member of the Tyee Club for six years. He told us he saved his two-week vacation and all his extra money for this annual event. His camper and vehicle were well used, and his clothes had the comfort of many years of wear. He had landed several fish too small to qualify, and had lost at least three that he feels would have made it. Was he discouraged? "Nah, not at all. It's somethin' I look forward to and it don't matter that I'm not some rich guy. Everybody has the same opportunity out there. When I make the Club I'll probably start doin' somethin' else...like goin' to Montana and try for a ten pound brown."

There's a lot of that same attitude around this place. Wealth or social position don't matter. It's the achievement that puts everyone on the same level. By all means don't be afraid to try it if you find yourself in the Campbell River region between mid-July and mid-September. Exciting fishing! Both the Tyee Pool and the Frenchman's Pool—where the two largest Tyee ever entered in club records were caught—can be fished with flies so I still drop by now and then to give it a go... Someday!

MORE CHINOOK—A RELIABLE METHOD

Throughout our trips in this book I have tried to stress the importance of having good boating skills and a solid, seaworthy boat whenever you challenge the ocean. Without question it would be suicidal to go anywhere on the open sea without a stable craft, and even in inland waters from Campbell River down to Puget Sound, light boats under 14-feet are considered marginal for safety reasons. The only exceptions are the dory-types used close to shore in rowing pools.

Maneuverable 16- to 24-foot open boats with some horsepower and stand-up center consoles are the preferred choice for fly fishing. This type of boat allows good vision, freedom of movement and room for casting. Not everyone can afford Boston Whalers or the other ego-boats in that class, and they really are not necessary. Welded aluminum hulls are very popular and make far more sense when beaching or pulling into rocky landings or launching from poorly maintained ramps. My Montauk has dings, chips and patches along its bottom that would only be minor dents or scrapes on a metal boat.

The sacrifice comes when bashing through waves or getting tossed around by rip tides. Plastic hulls are far heavier and "softer" riding than aluminum, and do possess a few more favorable safety factors like full foam floatation and no rivets or welds to work loose. My Whaler has performed flawlessly for over ten years and I certainly have high praise for it. Still, I can honestly say if I ever replace it my next ocean boat will almost surely be a metal deep-hull model. My little episode with the rock at Kingcome Inlet would have ended differently, I could have skidded and floated a lighter, less keeled boat; I wouldn't have to be so darned particular about cleaning up fish slobber and scrubbing floors so they stay sparkling white; and I could power grunge up onto gravel beaches without worrying about scraping off the gel coat bottom finish.

Because Campbell River is such a popular fishing area waters often have heavy boat congestion, with hot spots sometimes holding over 200 boats seemingly all within casting distance. Therefore, it is imperative that in addition to having a seaworthy craft—for *any* ocean use—you have at least minimal boating-traffic skills if you plan to be part of this confusion.

Most of the best Chinook areas north of Wilby Shoal are not conducive to fly casting. The tides usually run too strong, or the fish are too deep, or there are too many boats stacked together...or a dozen other reasons. But there are some good areas for flies in addition to Wilby that several of us have had success in. One is the stretch of water along Island Highway (Hiway 19) between what is called "Big Rock" about one mile south of the town of Campbell River down to Willow Point, a distance of about five miles or so. There are several boat launch sites along here and boat rentals as well.

Dense kelp beds are along the entire distance, and early in the year—April and May particularly, and sometimes in June—there are usually good numbers of feeder springs between eight and 12 or more pounds. A flood or ebb tide will move your boat parallel along the kelp just like a river drift and you can target cast into pockets with dry lines or use fast-sinking lines or shooting tapers to cast ahead of the boat, let it sink, and pick up the slack as you approach the fly. This method has caught me a lot of fish over the years, just as the fly begins to lift when the boat moves past. If you get a hit and miss it, you can strip out the line you have recovered, let the fly sink a bit and get another shot when the boat drifts far enough past to move the fly again.

One year over Easter weekend a friend and I launched his boat at Big Rock (you can't miss it!). It was chilly but the sun was out and the water looked like a mirror. A mild tide ran southward along the east shoreline where we were. We could see bottom all along the kelp banks and schools of herring in among the stalks. Perfect.

My fishing partner wasn't a fly fisher, he liked to use Buzz-Bombs, a local lure invented by Rex Field, father of Doug Field of Zzinger lure fame we'll talk about shortly. Like Zzingers, Buzz-Bombs have a line-size hole lengthwise through their center that allows them to slide and spin up and down the line, stopping against the hook. The difference is Buzz-Bombs are diamond shaped and spin more radically. Anyway, Ian's lures and my flies were quite compatible as we floated along the kelp.

The first fish we caught was a ten or 12 pound lingcod, just the right size for eating had it been legal. Lingcod season was/is closed for spawning at that time. We watched the fish open its mouth and inhale Ian's white Buzz-Bomb right on the bottom. Later we would use this clear visibility as an aid to pull lures and flies away from undesirable fish.

The next fish was much more fun. I was using a two-inch sparse pink and white polar bear hair creation on a full dry line with about a seven foot leader. I think my rod was a 9-foot for an 8-weight, my steelhead rod in those days. We had just passed a small school of herring right on the surface in an open pocket of kelp. I fired the fly in, let it sink for a few seconds, and then stripped as we slowly moved by the spot. There was a soft tap and I set the hook firmly into a fish. My rod thumped about three times then an eight or ten pound spring charged out of the water, cleared the kelp, hit the water and jumped again...and landed right inside our boat! There was a mad scramble as equipment, lunch, rain gear, oars and tackle flew everywhere. Ian finally grabbed the fish and heaved it back over the side—except my fly had come out. We cracked up. That poor little Chinook didn't know what had happened. He jumped three more times before we saw his tail for the last time.

Schooling feeder-Chinook usually stick close together so we motored back to the place I had hooked up and tied our boat to a kelp. Ian fished on the outside of the bed and I threw back inside among the herring. A dozen casts and I hooked another one. This guy stayed down and zigged around through the kelp for awhile before I had to break it off. My next few casts were upstream along the outside of the fronds but I couldn't control the fly coming towards me with the current so I cast the other direction and then stripped back. A sinking line or taper would have let the fly go deep and given it much more action when retrieved. But I was using a full dry line and my fly didn't get down and I was too lazy to change to a sinker. By late afternoon we had released several more lings and other bottomfish, and Ian killed a prime 12 pound spring to smoke for a wedding. I didn't touch another salmon.

Next morning it was windy and we couldn't see into the rippled water. I had changed to a WF9-weight Type III full sinking Cortland line with a short seven-and-a-half foot leader. Full-sinkers are a bugger to control in moving water, especially when wind and tidal current are running at opposites (I didn't have any shooting tapers then). Again we launched at Big Rock and started our drift south along the kelp, much slower this day because of the breeze holding us back. My attempts to distance-cast downstream into the wind were atrocious so I opted to roll-cast a shorter line then strip out additional amounts. This worked and after ten or a dozen casts I hooked what I thought was a ling right under the boat near bottom at about 30-feet. My rod bumped a few times then went limp. "Lost him..."

I began stripping quickly to get my fly in and see if it was OK when a pee-wee spring ripped up through the surface about 20-feet behind us and skittered across the water. My fly was visible in the corner of its mouth and about that same time I caught up with the fish. "Whoa...he's still on there!" The little

Chinook was spirited but no match for the rod I was using and promptly came to the boat, about six pounds. Three more on flies and five or six on Ian's Buzz-Bomb up to about 12 pounds over the next three hours marked this stretch as prime water early in the year.

Last April I repeated the routine by myself to see if feeder Chinooks still used these kelp beds as their nursery. Armed with my 9-foot 6-weight rod, a 220-grain lead-core head, and two-inch Firecrackers, I connected with a ten pound spring within a half hour, and lost two more over the next two hours. All is well.

STILL MORE CHINOOK

May and June are prime months for Chinook runs from Campbell River down as far as Bates Beach near Comox. This is usually calm water much like Puget Sound and big springs can be taken right next to shore wherever there is bait. Seal Bay, just south of Bates is often a hot spot around Memorial Day. Flies that match baitfish color seem to be more important than size with these runs, although in the shallow water—sometimes only 20- to 30-feet—springs can be skittish so casting must be accurate and the fly fisher must be fairly quiet.

My best encounter was an evening in 1990. I launched my 11-foot Zodiac at George Bates' resort, fired up the 9.9 and zipped 300-yards down to Seal Bay. Small two-ish pound bluebacks were dimpling the surface just out from the Bay so I rigged my 6/7-weight rod with a WF9F/S Type III 20 foot sink tip, 9-foot 0X leader and a sparsely tied size 8 pink and white polar bear hair fly. Springs weren't on the agenda, though three or four had been weighed-in the evening before. One was a real bell-ringer—a 32 pound Tyee.

It was warm and very calm and the tide was just reaching high slack as I drifted in on a herring school. I sat and watched for a moment to determine if there were any bluebacks harassing them. It was probably a bit early in the year for that, however. Blueback coho would probably still be on "pink" feed—krill and seed shrimp. Several gulls were hovering above, waiting to flop down on any bait pushed to the surface, and a couple hundred yards towards shore a harbor seal—namesake of this bay—its head bobbing was waiting for something to happen as well. A sloshing boil about 30-yards ahead got the birds excited. Then again, closer to me this time. I stripped out about 60- or 70-feet of line, straightened out the coils, and fired a cast in the general direction of the fish.

I wasn't expecting much, seeing only one fish roll, and in fact I was watching the seal when a thundering strike took the line right out of my fingers. My daily fishing diary states the fish ran off over 40-yards of line on the first run, stopped, I set the hook three or four times, and it ran another 25-yards. For sure it wasn't a blueback! Holding the rod high I leaned back and reeled. That far away the fish was only sluggish resistance with the line stretch and a soft rod. Halfway in it sounded. We had drifted out over about 75-feet of water and it went to the bottom and sulked awhile before again ripping out 30- or 40-yards, this time heading back towards the shallow bay.

Suddenly bait surrounded my boat and ten feet below two big springs burst through the school, then returned to pick up stunned herring. They didn't pay any attention to me. I got pumped just watching them. As my Chinook came in another one joined it, excited by the activity, then zipped past under my boat. My fish shied from the net, charged away about 30-feet and made a spectacular jump...and threw the hook! "Damn!" Choked, I just stood there for a minute, rod hand on my hip, shaking my head. It was a good 25 pound fish.

When I picked up the line to retrieve I was bewildered. There was solid opposition. I lifted the rod, still not quite comprehending, but when a clone to the spring I had just lost launched across the water the message was clear. It had taken my fly completely dead-drift—something Chinooks do with fair regularity by the way. I set up, more on instinct than on purpose, and the game was on.

This one I landed about 30 minutes later. The day was ending and even in the flat light of dusk its bright silver side sparkled. The unmistakable Chinook smell was heavy as I removed the fly, stabilized the fish for a moment, then watched it swim casually down into the dark water. It had been a great outing and a first: Two Chinooks on one cast.

OTHER SALMONIDS

Many of the runs of sockeye and pink salmon that move through Johnstone Strait in July and August also funnel down through Discovery Passage, but these scarcely get any notice with so much attention on Chinook and coho. Pinks can be caught from the fishing dock in Campbell River and in estuaries of various rivers south as far as Comox.

The shallow sand flats off Goose Spit just out from the mouth of the Puntledge River in Comox Harbour can be great in August and September for pink salmon on flies, but watch for closures here. I haven't fished this for several seasons, but I'm told it still produces.

And there are still a few coastal cutthroat in many of the stream mouths and river estuaries all along this stretch as well. This is all catch and release because there are so few, but catch the tide right and it is a good bet you can hook a few on size 10 Rolled Muddlers, a Royal Wulff or even a Coachman. You might even get surprised and nail a steelhead.

Short nailed a steelhead story: A few years ago I was teaching my son D.J. how to fly cast off the mouth of the Oyster River. It was high flood and there were quite a few cutthroat dimpling. I had on a Bob Borden pink and yellow cutthroat pattern and was showing him the routine of stripping it across the water so it made a slight wake. Ten-inch to 15-inch cutthroat would zero-in on it from 20- or 30-feet away and come like sharks. I was having so much fun "showing" him how, I got carried away. Finally, no doubt out of guilt, I cast and let the fly sit while I handed the rod over to my son. By the time I got him set the "floating" line had sunk a little and when he started to retrieve the fly went under and his line tightened. "I'm stuck, dad." He reefed back on the rod and at almost the same moment it slammed forward and line peeled out.

"Hey, I *got* one!" A fish that looked to be about two feet long came out of the water, twisting and thrashing, and charged across the surface of the tide pool. "Wow, it's a monster, dad." I was astounded. I'd never seen a cutthroat that big on this side of the Island. The fish had total control of the situation, but quickly burned itself out running around, and if I do say so, D.J. did a good job of hanging in there. When he brought it in, I was further astonished to see that it was a steelhead, about four-plus pounds with a clipped adipose fin, marking it as a hatchery fish.

"All right, D.J.! Nice job," but he had already released it and was winding up to cast.

GETTING THERE

The Courtenay/Comox/Campbell River region is along the same Vancouver Island BC Provincial Highway 19 as our trips to Port Hardy, Kyuquot, etc. Virtually every community along this stretch caters to fisherpersons.

As with fishing anywhere it is difficult to predict exactly when salmon will be around, but the months I have mentioned can usually be counted on and the weather during the summer is usually good on inland waters. Obtain marine charts "3594—Discovery Passage", and "3539—Quadra Island" for information about boating in the Campbell River region. Again, the address to write for marine charts is Canadian Hydrographic Service, P.O. Box 6000, Sidney, BC V8L 4B2.

FIVE

OUTER COAST — VANCOUVER ISLAND

KYUQUOT, B.C

$\mathcal{T}$he west coast of Vancouver Island faces the open Pacific and in some areas is as pristine and primitive as the coastline around the Queen Charlottes. Except for three settlements about one third of the way up the island—Bamfield, Ucluelet, and Tofino—the region north of this, although heavily exploited, is still largely undeveloped.

Seafaring native Indians had mastery of these waters for countless centuries, their war canoes and fishing craft transporting warriors and fishermen throughout the myriad of islands, coves, passes and inlets, and across exposed, open stretches of the sea. Early ships of discovery from Spain and England reported great wealth in the ocean and on land here, and subsequently, European and American adventurers, settlers, missionaries and sailors came seeking souls and wealth.

Ocean-going dugouts and giant war canoes have long been displaced by commercial and recreational craft. Chain saws and heavy equipment have replaced the sound of drums and songs, and only names of places remain to commemorate the heritage of native Indians: Clayoquot, Nootka, Klaskish, Nimpkish, Kyuquot...

There are few places on Vancouver Island where the impact of development is more striking than the region from Kyuquot Sound north to Checleset Bay. Steep hillsides have been clear-cut and scarred by logging roads. Massive slides occur with every rainfall. Once-fine spawning streams are now clogged and barren, and indigenous runs of anadromous fish such as steelhead and salmon have been decimated. If my comments sound like the proverbial broken record, then welcome to the west coast of North America, folks, where what you see is the way it is, and—in the words of the forest industry—if you don't like it...tough!

At this time there are four protected forest sites in the entire region: Tiny Rugged Point Marine Park and three small, isolated ecological reserves at Clanninick Creek, Tahsish estuary island, and the islands in Checleset Bay. Outside of these sites virtually every remaining tree in the Kyuquot region is calculated into cut allowances.

And before you label me a spotted owl lover or a tree-hugger, understand that I realize the need for logging and jobs, corporate profit, controlled use and development, and the meaning of sustained-yield. I also understand biodiversity, environmental conservation, simultaneous forest usage, social and cultural respect. The logging horrors here and in some other regions along the unpopulated coast show none of this. The socio-economic losses resulting from poor forest management are, in my opinion, far more costly to local residents, states and provinces than any financial value derived. What kind of image does this portray to outside visitors or to those of us who would come here to enjoy what is purported to be "our" forest heritage?

A few years ago I saw a TV documentary slated to be shown in Europe and Asia about the ecocatastrophe created by the timber industry in British

Columbia. One of the most devastating scenes shown from the air was this same Kyuquot region. Evidently the sponsors of the film—and I'm sorry I cannot remember what organization it was—had received no response from government to their requests for an investigation into "environmental crimes" and they decided to go global to seek international help for their cause. Apparently this, along with efforts by other groups, had some effect because in 1993 the Commission on Resources and the Environment was formed and charged with ensuring a "Protected Area" system for Vancouver Island.

Two close friends and I explored the Kyuquot (pronounced Ky-you-kwit) area together for the first time last summer. Our reaction to the landscape was predictable. "The bureaucrats and logging company executives who allowed this to happen should be hunted down and boiled in oil." I don't blame the loggers. They did what they were told to do. And I probably can't blame company managers either—they did what the government allowed. The resource should be utilized, but properly and with respect for all living things that would share it. There is no reason to strip steep terrain or to destroy living streams. My heart aches when I review my memory of this place and recall the stories the native people who still live here told me about what is was like before the logging companies came. Yet many from the village were on the payroll and participated in the destruction. Their hearts are also sad.

If you turn your eyes from the hillsides, however, there is still much that is beautiful here. The cold, clear Pacific is fragmented by hundreds of islands and reefs, which are home to countless sea birds and colonies of seals and sea lions. Vast kelp beds provide cover for schools of herring that attract coho and Chinook salmon. The smooth sand and gravel floor of the sound holds big halibut, and gray whales stop to feed on krill and other zooplanktons during their migrations from Mexico to Alaska and back. And sea otters, once hunted to the verge of extinction for their skins, have made a dramatic comeback, thanks to extraordinary transplant efforts.

Like Haida Gwaii, Kyuquot is not a place for novice or unprepared boaters. It faces the open ocean, where 30-knot winds and cold dense fog can hit anytime and where rocks and jagged reefs are not all charted. We were fortunate to have Jerry Lang and Rupert Wong of West Coast Expeditions as hosts during our five-day stay. Both men are professional marine biologists and outdoor specialists who have been conducting wilderness adventure trips to this remote area since 1974. After our time with them, we gained a heightened awareness of the beauty and fragility of the unique ecosystem prevalent along the entire west coast.

Our travel here took on a strange dichotomy of emotions. The avenue to and from the staging area, where we would launch our boat and leave our vehicle, was over logging roads built years earlier to haul out the timber torn from hillsides we would later mourn. On the way in, my air-conditioned Suburban closed out the suffocating dust that filled my boat and permeated everything in it. We launched from a crude ramp in its fourth year of "temporary replacement" for the broken main ramp, and flew across glassy water nine miles to our island camp. Each of us was too preoccupied with his own thoughts to perceive the dust cloud boiling out behind and swirling into our hair and ears and up our noses and down our necks. That night we would eat gritty food, wipe down dusty gear, sneeze in our sleeping bags and have to shake out every piece of clothing, but for now all we could see was the wonderment of this new adventure and a rose-colored world.

The settlement of Kyuquot is split into two sites: the general town with its long, high dock, commercial fishing repository and other mercantile ventures is on a small island; and the Indian village, located beneath the scarred hills on main Vancouver Island is just across the channel. It's a busy place from spring until fall when fish are running and there is some tourism. But it can only be reached by boat or plane, and there is little information about the area. I suspect many of the local people are just as happy there isn't more of an invasion each summer, even though it would pump dollars into the community. Salmon runs are not strong here, tending to move on after only a few days. But when they are around fishing can be spectacular.

There is a motel of sorts in Kyuquot, along with a restaurant, general store, fuel dock and at least one bed-and-breakfast, and as this is being written a new destination lodge is being constructed that should be ready by summer of 1995 (much to the disappointment of many who consider Kyuquot to be their own "secret" place). We opted to stay at West Coast Expeditions' camp on Spring Island. The tents were comfortable, and when Rupert or Jerry cooked the meals, food was excellent. And the cost was very reasonable. Anyone planning a trip here *must* secure accommodations ahead (see "Getting There" at the end of this section). You can camp on your own, but most of the land and islands are Indian Reserve and permission to camp is not always granted. Check with the band members in town.

We spent the first afternoon on the water getting to know the area. My last trip here was in 1985 and, while obviously none of the islands or landmarks had moved, I remembered very little. As we usually do in a new area, we searched out fishy-looking places and checked for bait and bigger fish on my sounder. We're all fanatical fly fishers, but sometimes we also use lightweight conventional gear and probe with Zzingers, a sliding lure made by our friend Doug Field in Courtenay, BC. This often eliminates fly gear getting ratched by dog sharks or other undesirable critters, and usually lets us know quickly what is down there.

Our first fish was a 25 pound halibut which we released. Halibut were the only fish we considered taking back with us and, though we would spend many hours fishing for them during the days that followed, this would be the only one we would hook. In addition, we would release dozens of lingcod, kelp greenling, copper, black, china and quillback rockfish, a giant sculpin (a *real* first for me on a fly), several mackerel, and a couple we couldn't identify. Just before going in that first evening we also happened on a large school of squid which had been forced to the surface, and we managed to snag several for dinner before they disappeared. Try *that* on a fly.

Squid are also responsible for another phenomenon that occurs every summer in these waters. They spawn on a shallow shelf on the shoreward side of the channel across from the light house. The story is, females attach a sack of eggs to the sea floor or to rocks in about 50-feet of water, and the males stick around to guard the nest until eggs hatch. Normal spawning in this part of the country takes place in May or June. I don't know the gestation period for squid—and no one I asked could tell me—but their are squid here right into August so I assume it takes about that long until the young are mobile(?). I have accidentally snagged spawn sacks at that time also. Fish come to feed on the squid which are normally about eight or nine inches long. It is not unusual to catch halibut over 100 pounds and big Chinooks that are stuffed with them. Not too many people are aware of this annual sym-biotic ritual between squid, fish, and man, and I can't honestly validate the part about male "guards," but fishermen who understand what is going on do very well here. I discovered it by accident in early August 1983.

Short squid story: I was casting for salmon near a kelp bed and not having any action. On one throw I let my line go down while I had a slurp of coffee and when I started my retrieve there was an odd sort of hit. My reflexes were faster in those days and I sat up immediately and felt a little twitch at the end of my line. Stripping in quickly I was amazed to see a squid with tentacles wrapped around my fly. While it was dangling at the surface, not 12-feet from the boat, there was a loud sucking-champing sound as a big Chinook came up underneath and inhaled it like a monster trout taking a mayfly. My line was all over the boat and under my feet so needless to say I didn't have it on very long, but it did set the stage for some great action over the next few days, including a 108 pound halibut caught by my friend Barry Blois on an 8-weight fly rod (using a live squid).

That phenomenon doesn't last long, however, and as Doug and George and I pulled our hooks through the school of squid that evening in July I wondered if this school was part of the annual ritual. Unfortunately it proved not to be.

The next morning while Doug slept in, George and I hiked to the site of the old Loran station on the west side of Spring Island. Built during WW II by the Army Corps of Engineers it served as an electronic beacon for years until permanent sites were established at Alert Bay and Williams Lake, BC, which are still in use pending probable replacement by the new GPS satellite locator technology.

Although swampy, Spring Island has no running freshwater nor any developed springs. There is also no evidence of big cedar trees, so historically it was probably not used by native people. The flat, half-acre raised portion where we camped is actually a huge gravel pile barged in and dumped by the engineers for their own camp during construction of the Loran site. It is ideally located on the leeward side of the island on a large bay and provides excellent drainage when it rains.

After breakfast Rupert led us to Rugged Point Marine Park a few miles down the coast to look for a gray whale that had been feeding there the week before. It had apparently resumed its journey, so we moved on to Grassy Island to view fossils of shelled creatures embedded in solid rock dating back 105 million years. This is Reserve land and while there is plenty to see, removal of any materials is prohibited. Further along we passed a raft of several sea otters sleeping entwined together, and at Volcanic Island we watched tufted puffins flying to nests with perfectly arranged rows of herring hanging from their short, brightly colored bills.

At Higher Island things got interesting. My sounder showed a flat, sand bottom at 70-feet which stretched to the base of a high, rocky cliff. Occasionally during dives Rupert had seen halibut estimated at 50 pounds here. I let the boat drift and Rupert, Doug and George each put down a different lure. Rupert was the first to hook up. His line started peeling out and all of us had the same mindset: halibut. It was obviously a good fish, but when a Chinook jumped only 40-feet away we were astonished. About that same time, Doug also hooked a spring and the fire drill was on. I couldn't contain myself and cast my sinking head, though I didn't really expect to get down there. Before it was over we released two nice springs, two coho, and a variety of bottomfish. A very rewarding day, but no halibut.

That night we ate a gourmet seafood stirfry of squid, scallops, mussels, sea cucumber, and rockfish prepared in a wok on a Coleman stove by Jerry.

Garnished with a variety of edible kelp it was a feast for kings. Later we sat by a fire and George and I sipped scotch and slurred toasts to the ghosts we could hear on the soft ocean breezes until it was time to crawl across the sand to our tents. It was great.

COHO OR CHINOOK? THE MAGIC OF THIS PLACE

We headed north towards Brooks Peninsula the next day to visit abandoned village sites of the original Nuu-chah-nulth native people. These very special sites are amazingly well-preserved and carefully protected from outsiders. About halfway there we ran into the teeth of a 25-knot wind and had to turn around. We stopped to cast awhile inside Double Rock on the way back, but it was just too rough and we settled instead for some good video footage and stills of the large stellar sea lion colony there.

Back in calmer water inside Light House Island, coho were ripping through a large school of herring. We tied the boat to several bulbs of kelp and set up for what we were sure would be great action.

Bob Jones had tied me a dozen new Firecrackers, George wanted to strip cast small live herring with a light fly rod, and Doug tried a new seven-foot G. Loomis graphite rod with a two ounce Zzinger. We all hooked fish within minutes, and released a dozen or more coho between eight and 12 pounds over the next hour—very large for the middle of July. Then, right at high-slack tide, as quickly as it started, the action was over. Herring were still under us but the coho absolutely disappeared.

While we ate lunch, compared notes and reloaded film, George had left his line in the water. His rod was rigged with 12-pound-test leader, a one ounce weight, size 6 single hook and a small herring. We all saw his rod slowly bend at the same time. Thinking dogfish, George grabbed the rod without even taking the sandwich out of his mouth—just as a monster spring exploded across the water.

George's little 5-weight fly rod had pretty well been tested to the limit on coho. Now he was hooked to a Chinook that was at least 40 pounds. "Not a chance in hell, George!" was all the encouragement Doug and I offered.

But he stayed with it. Every time the fish ran long, George would say, "Well, I guess that's it!" When it nearly spooled him, he coaxed some line back. When it jumped and thrashed and threw its head at the surface, he slackened the line so the light leader wouldn't part. When the reel got hot and started to bind at one point, he dunked it in water. Once when the fish ran into the kelp, he wailed, "That's *really* it, it's all over." But he led the fish back the same way it went in. In short, he did everything right and after nearly an hour we realized he was going to land it.

The down side of using light gear is the possibility big fish, if fought too long, will exhaust themselves beyond recovery. Unfortunately that happened with this great fish. We tried for over half an hour to revive it, but it was no use. It weighed 42 pounds.

We landed several springs that afternoon—two of them in the 30 pound range—and were able to release them all. I had a memorable struggle with an eight pounder that took my fly just as I was lifting it to cast and my line ended up in a Charlie Brown-like kite string explosion around my feet, motor, gas tank, and George. The fish ran and George and I were pulled together like we'd been roped (I *like* George, but...). It took about two minutes to get untangled, and all the time the fish was charging against the line. We got it sorted out and I ripped the fish to the boat, popped the hook out and got him back on his way. Everyone had a good laugh.

Our first realization that the springs were gone was when we started catching coho again. And it was like that in the following days as well. We would tie to kelp near a school of baitfish and catch coho until high-slack tide. Then the coho quit and the springs came on. Never in all my years of salmon fishing had I experienced that situation, nor have I since. In the three days we fished there, we did not catch a coho while the Chinooks were present.

On our last afternoon I hooked a huge spring right at the boat that George got a good look at before it ran. He estimated it was over 60 pounds. It was one of those "Holy smut!"-sized fish. It never stopped and the hook pulled out after about 200-yards. Believe it or not, I was relieved.

Between the wind and the salmon fishing we never did get to the aboriginal village. We should have, but there are lots of things we "should" do. We did gain far more from this visit to Kyuquot than just good fishing. This place is spectacular, even now after all that has been done to it. Logging will likely continue unabated until there is no wilderness left on Vancouver Island. That appears to be the plan. When everything is gone, only then will it be apparent what has been lost. Certainly there are not the same global implications as losing the South American rain forests, but for the sake of future generations some of this must be left.

(The good news is, my friend and fishing partner, Doug Dennett has returned to Kyuquot with his family each year since the trip described here and in the first week of August 1994 he hit more and bigger fish than we did, under the *same* circumstances).

SOCKEYE

There are excellent runs of sockeye that move along the coast from Winter Harbour north of Kyuquot, all the way down past Tofino in July and August each year. These stay well out from shore, however, until they enter Barkley Sound heading for home rivers and it is very difficult to locate them unless the commercial fleet is fishing. I have never gone after them, but a few sports fishers who have say it can be exciting.

One story I heard was about two fellows from California who motored 20 miles out from Ucluelet after sockeye and ended up catching a 20-pound albacore tuna. They found an incredible amount of fish and bird activity out in "blue" water and cast into a wild feeding frenzy. They hooked several fish that absolutely tore up their salmon gear! The one they landed was on a stiff 13-weight rod and a big billfish fly they had used in South America. I guess it was stimulating to say the least. I have heard of commercial guys getting into some exotic fish well out off the west coast, but never a fly fisher doing it. Sounds like great fun to me. I'd try it...

GETTING THERE

Kyuquot is on the northwest coast of Vancouver Island reached only by boat from Fair Harbour or by float plane. The last place for fuel is at Woss, about 80 miles north from Campbell River on Provincial Highway 19. About 13 or 14 miles further along Highway 19 is the turnoff to Zeballos. This is the beginning of the gravel logging road system that leads to Fair Harbour, a distance of about 60 miles.

Trailering boats over 2000 pounds is not recommended because of the condition of the road and the poor launch ramp. I have seen large boats put in there, but I sure wouldn't want to try it. I also recommend a good, tight-fitting boat cover or everything you have in your boat will be covered with dust unless it's raining. Then it will just be mud.

As mentioned, you must secure accommodations if you decide to go there. The best bet is to send for the Ministry of Tourism Accommodations and Travel Guide mentioned in earlier "Getting There" sections. A current issue might list the new lodge, motel and B & B there, but it may not. You can contact Rupert Wong at West Coast Expeditions, 1348 Ottawa Street, West Vancouver, BC V7T 2H5—phone 604/926-1110. This is a camp situation, but it is quality. WCE provides tents and meals, and their programs are primarily involved with ecological studies, marine biology, and ocean kayaking. During good weather it's a good program for families with kids over ten as well. Lots to see and do. My good friend Doug went back with his wife and 14 year-old son the week after our fishing trip and had an excellent time. They spent quality time together, plus he was able to get off by himself fishing once or twice a day while they did other things. West Coast Expeditions picks up patrons at Fair Harbour and returns them when the holiday is over. Rupert can also give you names and addresses of possible alternatives if his camp is full.

It is also possible to camp at Fair Harbour and boat each day to the areas mentioned—about nine to twelve miles—but you would have to be totally self-contained. There are no facilities of any kind there, including no water or restrooms. Fair Harbour is basically just a large gravel parking lot used by logging companies and residents of Kyuquot. Boat fuel and containers of water can be obtained at Kyuquot. And fishing is sometimes good right in Kyuquot Sound and Kashutl Inlet.

Fishermen need to take their own boats. The region around Kyuquot would be all right for cartoppers because there are many islands and coves to duck into, but getting it *out* there is kind of dicey. You must cross a wide bay that can be nasty in a wind. For that reason I wouldn't recommend it unless you can travel with another boat. Before I got my Whaler, I had a 15-foot Alumacraft with a 35 hp outboard. I used that boat all over the Pacific, from Mexico to northern BC, usually alone. While in Kyuquot in 1983 I ran over a plastic bag that covered the water intake of my engine and toasted it. Without Jerry Lang to tow me six miles back to camp and later ten miles to Fair Harbour it would have been a long walk. Obtain nautical charts 3682 and 3683 and study them.

Fishing equipment is fairly standard for this area. You probably won't get into any runs of salmon other than coho and Chinook, but the Chinook can be big. I would plan on taking a 6- or 8-weight rod and a 9- or 10-weight with the usual saltwater reels and lines. You might also want to take a 12-weight rod and try for halibut if you go in the first two weeks of August. Have some squid patterns (Dan Blanton in San Jose, California ties the best one I've seen) and get them down to the bottom along the channel that runs north and south between Spring Island and the light house. You'll see it. Halibut will be there, and if you hook one, don't forget our friend Charlie's trick of backing off about 100-feet and lifting their heads to plane them to the surface rather than sitting over them trying to pry them off the bottom.

NOOTKA ISLAND

About 40 miles south of Kyuquot as the whale swims is the south end of Nootka Island and Friendly Cove, an inviting name until one reads the history of this place.

In 1803 a Yankee two-mast square rigger, the *Boston* out of Massachusetts anchored in the cove where the native village of Yoquot had been occupied continuously for over 4000 years. The captain and crew were bartering with the Nootka Indian clan of that area, the Mowachaht, and their chief, Maquinna for sea otter skins and other provisions. Because of plundering and murder by earlier Spanish traders, and, no doubt, for something this crew did as well, Maquinna had the captain and crew of the *Boston* killed. There is no record of whether police ever took action, but within a few years diseases had exacted a certain revenge for the deaths, much the same as befell the Haida.

Last time I was here Yoquot and Friendly Cove were deserted except for a native family living in the village area, and another family tending the light house on the point protecting the cove. Since Canada turned most of its light houses on auto-pilot even they may be gone by now. And until recently I had rarely seen other recreational fishing boats here other than a few from nearby Nootka Island Fish Camp and the odd charter boat that comes down from Gold River, unusual for a place of such scenic wonder and reachable fishing along Vancouver Island. Still "undiscovered" I guess. It sure isn't because fishing is poor.

This is isolated, rugged country—definitely off the beaten track—but at the same time one of the most strikingly beautiful places anywhere along the coast. Over the hill from the old village site and across a "sea" of perpetually blooming wildflowers is a long, white-sand beach, and while the usual distasteful logging scars are evident in the background, it is easy to daydream about what it must have been like when Maquinna walked here. Seaward from Friendly Cove around to Maquinna Point and on up as far as Bajo Point the sea and land are spectacular. Coves, reefs, rocky cliffs, kelp, and forests that touch the sea(!). This is salmon water, and for the fly fisher that can stand the rigors of the open ocean—swells, breakers that crash across the reefs, surges that run up and back along rock faces and around the kelp beds—it will consistently produce, especially in July and August.

If weather or sea conditions are too rough, there is good fishing right in front of Friendly Cove and north up along Cook Channel. There are nearly always herring in the bays and around islands up through this area and across the channel in the islands there, and coho and springs. Further north is Kendrick Inlet and Tahsis Inlet. Big springs often move up here on their way to spawning streams, but read fishing regulations for area closures in August in many of the inlets and bays in this area (and elsewhere on Vancouver Island).

If weather or waves are really bad out on the ocean or if fog has rolled into the sound, the north point of Bligh Island across from Tlupana Inlet and the rock shoals and reefs in this area can be dynamite in late July and August, and sometimes into September. It is easy fishing and unquestionably much safer than out on the big water, but I find it very confining especially when overcast. Steep hills, heavy brush, clear-cuts...it just doesn't have the feel of ocean fishing. But there are Chinooks here and coho move through as well. As usual, find kelp and bait and go for it. Cast all day when the weather is dark or if the water is rippled.

Across Nootka Sound from Friendly are more beaches, coves, rock points and the long southward-jutting Hesquiat Peninsula that ends at Estevan Point. This is also fishing country with huge, marvelous kelp beds and reefs but it is highly exposed to the open ocean, swells, and any winds blowing in from the north and west.

About 50 boat-miles southeast of here down the coast are the protected waters of Clayoquot Sound, and another 30 miles beyond that are the prolific waters of Barkley Sound, highly desirable regions we will visit later.

From Yoquot Beach, where Nootka longhouses once stood, you can see the reefs and kelp beds just offshore where big Chinook and coho runs first touch when they move into Nootka Sound from the rocks at Bajo Reef. This is tricky water and fishing it requires exact positioning of your boat so you aren't washed onto rocks. We'll have a session on reef fishing later that will open your eyes. It can be exciting fishing along a shelf that averages 60- to 90-feet—perfect depth for salmon that will come to the kelp for herring. A little farther out into the sound the water drops off 140- to 240-feet in a hurry. The bottom out there is mostly sand, and big halibut wait on the bottom. Lingcod and rockfish are closer in among the rocks. There is always great expectation in this place.

COHO

I made the 25 mile run down Muchalat Inlet from the town of Gold River early on an August morning. Launching in Gold River estuary at road's end (just past the mill) the chilly run to Friendly Cove took me less than an hour. I don't particularly like doing this trip alone, especially in the dark. Not many boats go down here unless a good run is happening and then locals from Gold River will. Otherwise it can be a very lonely trip.

Sometimes wild winds funnel up and down the channel making travel slow and bumpy, and if fog has pushed in past the opening of the sound it could be a wasted trip. I didn't have a course plotted into my Loran memory for this area. But neither of these adverse conditions were present this day, although strong afternoon winds were a probability because it had been clear and hot for several days.

It was light as I rounded Anderson Point and headed the last leg straight down Zuchiarte Channel. Only a slight ripple moved on the water as I rounded the south point of Bligh Island and set a course for Yoquot Point three miles away. Flat swells coasted in as I approached the rocks and kelp beds in front of Maquinna Point.

I sat for awhile, gently rising and falling with the surges, looking for moving fish. Not much going on yet. I motored to several spots I had fished before, looking for bait or some action. Nothing. With my line trailing out the back I slowly motor-mooched among the rocks and reefs closer in, watching the sun come up and listening to the surf hit the shore. Birds were talking and overhead a jet was heading north. Peaceful. A solid strike brought me around and I glanced back just in time to see a coho clear the water and rip towards the open sound. Another jump and it was gone. I went back and saw a small school of herring in some kelp. "This must be the place," it looked good. I tied up and cast for about half an hour. Nobody else was home.

Just east of a big rock near the point something was thrashing the hell out of the water. As I pulled up a herring ball about the size of my boat was protruding several inches out of the water, boiling. I didn't mean to but I carried right through the middle of it. A *big* dogfish shark swam slowly out of the side of the pack, dorsal fin cutting the surface, jaws munching like some maniacal eating machine, herring parts and blood oozing out with every chew. I got chills just watching and visions of you-know-what-movie flashed through my mind. It was grotesque. Nature at its most colorful. There had to be several more below the school to keep it pushed up like that. I didn't cast...no guts. I waited until my boat drifted clear, then powered up and moved around to the seaward side of the rock. More kelp a bit further along. And more herring, a large school this time. I pulled into a notch and tied up.

The sun was bright on the water now, and I doubted there would be any salmon on top, but I cast to the side of the herring school anyway, let my line sink for 30-seconds then started my usual slow two-foot-long "Chinook" retrieve. This time I was alert when a soft tap vibrated up my rod. Pointing my tip I stripped quickly and lifted hard when I felt the fish. A bright, silver coho erupted right next to me, crashed back down and immediately charged under the boat and came up again on the other side. I jammed my rod deep in the water and walked the line past the motor and out the back. It was running now, straight away from me. Then a sharp-angle left turn, another jump and away it went in a wide sweep around the front of the boat. It wasn't the big Chinook I was hoping for but what a great fish! Two tries barehanded and I finally resorted to the net to subdue this guy, about eight pounds.

Looking past him into the kelp I saw two more charging the herring. Hook out, quick swish back and forth to revive the fish, check for nicks in the leader—the heck with it. Cast. Wham! Two fish in two casts, only this one went straight into the kelp and out the other side. I had outsmarted myself. A right turn towards deep water, a jump and it was all over. I reeled in and put on another tippet and a Chinook-sized four-inch Firecracker. Two dozen casts with no action and it was time to move again. I considered going across and fishing around Discovery Point and Camp Beach. It was calm enough and the swells still weren't big. But right where I was had always rated as one of the best stretches. I talked myself into staying on this side. Back towards Yoquot Beach, closer in this time.

Halfway across an open stretch was a little kelp bed I had never noticed. No rocks protruding anywhere so that meant fairly shallow water. I tied up to the last frond, drifted back out over a dark-water drop-off, and brought out my big stick—the 12-weight! A 550-grain head with 12-feet of leader and tippet was already on my Fin-Nor. I loop-tied a Polar Herring and lobbed it out about 70-feet, stripping out line as it plummeted towards the bottom. My sounder showed a solid, flat bottom at 59 feet and there was a slight tide running so I allowed two minutes for the line to get down there. It looked barren, not even a bump on the floor. I slowly lifted my line, reeling slack on the down stroke. Several lifts later I got a quick thump and then heavy bucking as line peeled back out. Pump, reel, pump, reel, lift, reel. Slowly a shape materialized below me and I recognized the ugly smile of a lingcod. Primitive, slant-eyed and toothy, it was about ten or 12 pounds finning on the surface.

I was considering what to do with it when an even larger shape loomed underneath it and grabbed it sideways. This sucker was huge, at least 40 pounds. No way! I leaned back as hard as I could and didn't budge them. Using my rod tip I slapped the water. Still no response. The smaller fish was locked in the big guy's mouth (actually big female when they are that big). Then head shakes and the little one started to struggle. Again I reefed against them and succeeded in lifting the big one's head to the surface. Finally it let go and headed back down. I grabbed my line and towed the smaller fish to the boat. The fly came out easily—it never did penetrate past the barb—and the fish rolled on its side, revealing two rows of punctures back and belly. Nothing serious. It flipped water in my face and headed towards the bottom. I smirked and wiped off my glasses. So much for deep-lining.

It was closing in on noon when there would be a slack tide. I needed to find a place with bait and some salmon. Almost like magic a fish rolled on the far side of the kelp and herring showered to all sides. It was a good fish.

FEEDER CHINOOK

I stowed my big rod and checked the leader on my 9-weight. I quickly replaced it, tied on a 12-pound-test tippet, a new Firecracker, and cast across the kelp towards the spot I'd seen the fish roll. There is no reason in the world to believe this, but I swear my fly didn't even hit the water and a short sumo-size spring had it. I could see it slowly contorting, head to tail, side to side just under the surface. Then it shot straight ahead for about 30-feet, turned towards me and flexed again. You can guess what happened then. The fly just fell out of its mouth. *I forgot to set the hook!* It was at least a 20 pound spring. Unbelievable.

After a couple dozen more casts I started to consider heading back. I was getting tired and sunburned, and a stiff breeze was beginning to ruffle the water that meant if it continued, it would be a rough ride home. With my mind far from this place, I got another tap-tap. I stripped. Nothing. Tap-tap. Strip again. Again, nothing. I kept the fly moving and just as I relaxed, wham! A fat little spring about ten or 12 pounds boiled the water and charged away. A good fight and it came to the boat. Bright, clean, eager to be released, like a kid trying to get out of being bathed. I watched it dart away and after checking my leader, cast again. Three more casts and its brother came to my fly. Same scenario. This was great.

I hooked four more in the next hour and landed two, all the same size. Feeder springs we call them, resident to the area and probably getting ready to head off on their big adventure in the open sea. Hopefully these learned a tiny lesson of survival this day: "Don't bite those damn spinny-things." I looked around. Not another soul in sight. Just the bright passive sea and me. Further out was a black line. Wind. Time to leave.

It caught me just as I came out of King Passage into Muchalat and pushed me towards home. I slowed down and enjoyed the scenery. It was a straight shot from here.

SUMMARY

"If I had to choose one place..." as the saying goes, this might well be it. Not because it has the "best" fishing (it doesn't), but because I enjoy solitude and being on the edge of adventure. There is so much yet to be discovered about this region. It will take some exploration time and much patience, but I believe the surface has hardly been scratched by sports fishermen here. (Update: I made this trip again on Saturday, July 23, 1994 and although there weren't many fish there were over 100 sports fishing boats...many with WN registration letters. I believe Nootka is being discovered as we read this, and that's OK).

Inside Nootka Sound in the protected inlets and bays and around the islands there seem to always be a few wild salmon, though most runs are "produced" now, usually resident fish—feeder springs and small coho— staying close to home until they are ready to begin their migration. You may catch *more* fish in say May and June, but fish will be larger in July and August as new runs move into their home waters before spawning.

On both sides of the entrance don't be surprised if you hit halibut, lingcod and uncountable numbers of rockfish—I didn't even mention how many of these are taken every trip! If you get bored from not catching salmon, take on these no-brainers. Halibut and lingcod aren't much for fighting—they can sure as hell pull, though—but some of the rockfish are fun, particularly black rocks (called black bass) which will run, rip, jump and tear. They are all around the rocky reefs wherever there is kelp and are very nice eating.

Outside the sound, northwest and southeast along the coast, are some of the wildest waters you will ever see. But they can be full of fish, schools moving along from Oregon, Washington, BC and Alaska, following age-old migration routes and feed.

Saltwater Reels. Top: mooching reel. Right: Pflueger Supreme. Bottom: Fin-Nor and G. Loomis Rod.

Shooting taper line system for saltwater.

Baitfish patterns; the top fly is over 7 inches long.

Squid and shrimp patterns.

Firecrackers, created by Bob Jones, Courtenay, B.C.

"Experimental" Mylar patterns created by Bob Jones.

Charlie cleaning halibut. Queen Charlotte Islands, 1993.

Stomach contents of halibut—severed clam necks!

Doug's Chinook is released in front of spectators. Queen Charlotte Islands, 1993.

RCMP Marine patrol boat and the M.V. Driftwood. *Queen Charlotte Islands, 1993.*

Early morning on Queen Charlotte Lodge dock, 1993.

New Long House and totem in Old Masset Village, Queen Charlotte Islands, 1992.

Tow Hill in Naikoon Provincial Park, Queen Charlotte Islands, 1992.

George with a coho kept for the BBQ. Kyuquot, 1993.

Herring ball. Kyuquot, 1993.

George's coho on the grill. Kyuquot, 1993.

"Camping" on Spring Island (West Coast Expeditions). Kyuquot, 1993.

Stellar sea lion colony on Double Rock. Kyuquot, 1993.

Ravages of logging evident on hills behind Kyuquot Village, 1993.

Dick Close's Weigh West Marine Resort, Tofino, 1994.

The "Glory Hole"—surge fishing water. Tofino, 1994.

Author shooting side-arm for salmon. Tofino, 1994.

Robert H. Jones

Author (left) and Dave Lornie releasing a coho. Tofino, 1994.

S A L M O N   T O   A   F L Y

Dave Lornie with a black (bass) rockfish—one of dozens caught. Tofino, 1994.

Even so, there is no reliable "best time" when salmon will be here, or where they will be. There are always moderating factors such as size of the springtime herring spawn in local kelp beds that will determine the availability of bait through summer, or success of the salmon spawns in nearby streams, or El Niño.

Tides nearly always have a strong effect on fishing also, and in summer there are some wide tidal movements around Vancouver Island (there are "normal" tides as well that are more timely spaced). In each 24-hour period there will be at least one very low tide followed in approximately seven or eight hours by a much higher tide. The next low, often only three or so hours later, may not drop more than two or three feet, and the second high of the day will only rise a few feet above that. The best "bite" is often the hour before this second high or low point, the time during the slack—before it changes—and then the hour following.

For springs it can be especially good if those high or low slack periods coincide with early morning or late evening, when the sun is low or not on the water. If it's overcast—and it often is out on the west coast—a strong bite can occur even in mid-day, although even springs will sometimes feed in bright sunlight as occurred during our trip to Kyuquot. The short of it is— and this is not a cop-out—you *never* really know for sure. The last comment I will make about tides is, *depending on the area* (the old "generalization" cop-out), extreme high-to-low or low-to-high movement sometimes really puts a damper on fishing. An entire chapter could be written about the effects of tidal movement on how good or bad fishing is or has been or will be. My point is, tides are important and it pays to find out about them for the area you will be in.

I have also mentioned weather and its effect on our travels. Everywhere along the west coast weather is the big equalizer. My friend Ralph Shaw calls it "The Great Conservationist" because when storms rage or winds blow or fog inhibits, no one fishes. Just use common sense. When it's nasty or foggy, stay inside and fish protected waters. Or play golf. When you get outside on the big water, use extreme caution. Watch for weather changes—which can happen quickly—and travel with other boats whenever possible (skip the whenever part—*always* travel with a buddy or other craft going your direction), and use a professional guide service for a day or two until you get familiar with a new region. I'm a great one for giving advice I don't follow, yet even with all my ocean experience and boating skills I will always try to link-up with someone who knows the area before I strike out on my own. The Pacific usually lives up to its name, but it pays to remember this side of

Vancouver Island didn't earn its reputation as "The Graveyard of the Pacific" by chance!

Obtain nautical chart 3664 for Nootka Sound.

GETTING THERE

Even considering all the cautions, I honestly don't understand why more people don't come here. It is certainly easier to get to than Kyuquot, and fly fishing is as good as anywhere I have fished. Take Provincial Highway 28 from Campbell River and keep going. It will end at the boat ramp in Gold River just past and across from the pulp mill in the river estuary. It's only about 60 miles from Campbell River, but the road is narrow and winding, so allow at least two hours if towing a boat. You'll pass some spectacular scenery (and some scarred-up stuff) and follow one of the best steelhead rivers on the Island—the Gold—for many miles. There is a campground in town for self-contained units. This program means boating down to the fishing area and back each day, but there can be good fishing along the way. Check locally on where the "runs" are.

Camping is also allowed in Friendly Cove (though there may be a charge), and there are a number of coves and beaches around that provide safe harbor—as long as you are familiar with ocean camping techniques. Because of tides along the outer coast you could wake up with your boat high and dry, or much farther from shore than anticipated. Or with a wet tent if you misjudge the high water line.

Short high and dry Story: An acquaintance joined us one year near the Bunsby Islands and because he didn't have a tent he decided to sleep in his boat (plus he snored so we didn't want him near us). He anchored a couple hundred feet out, lifted the outboard engine, and crawled under his boat tarp. Next morning the boat was sitting on top of a rock about six feet above water. We had to go get him for breakfast. *Know* the tides for the area you'll be (every sports store will have a book of tide tables available at no charge). Plus have a nautical chart that shows such spots.

There are several ways to secure your boat while camping. Use a solid anchor with a float, and rig a long rope pulley—like a revolving clothes line—to retrieve your boat. If the boat is small enough, beach it above high tide every night. Or, anchor deep and use a small raft or boat as a shuttle. If your boat is tied directly to the anchor (as compared to tying up to the float), be sure you allow enough slack line for ten- to 15-foot tidal fluctuations. It definitely won't do to lose your boat in this country.

Camping is very enjoyable along the coast as long as the weather cooperates. There are many creeks flowing into inlets and water from these can be used for washing and cooking, but take drinking water with you, as well as all provisions. Emergency gas can probably be purchased from a fish camp or another boat, but don't count on it. Also, if you do decide to camp out around Friendly Cove, you must get permission from the Mowachaht band office in Gold River and pay a small fee (get a receipt and take it with you).

There are a couple of other launch and camp sites at Tahsis and Cougar Creek, which are closer to the fishing than Gold River, but I don't know enough about these to recommend them. And last time I was there an Infocentre tourism service was operating in Gold River. Call BC Tel information for Gold River (area code 604) and ask about it. They would be able to put you in contact with fishing guides and other services, as well as the current situation with camping on native land—and whether or not there are fish down there! And there is always the BC Provincial Ministry of Tourism guide mentioned several times.

For the adventurer or pioneer among you, *this is the place*. I'll see you there!

CLAYOQUOT SOUND

This is the heart of Nuu-Chah-Nulth (original people) territory. Here the Ahousaht, Hesquiaht, Tlaoquiaht, Toquaht and Ucluelet are the indigenous seafaring tribes of the region. From its northern boundary at Flores Island south to Tofino Inlet, Clayoquot (pronounced Clack-kwit) Sound has more than four dozen streams and rivers pouring into it capable of sustaining salmonid spawning runs. Vast shallow backwater tidal flats support thousands of acres of grasses, kelp and other aquatic plants that shelter thick populations of mussels, dungeness and rock crabs, waterfowl, herons, herring, seed shrimp and planktons, and provide a nutrient-rich nursery for young salmonids.

Much of this region has so far been spared the ravages of rip-and-tear logging and many steep mountainsides and deep watersheds are pristine. There are logging scars to be sure, but with the Long Beach Unit of Pacific Rim National Park along the outer coast and up to 800,000 visitors flooding through here each year, the timber companies are on their best behavior. They *can* do it right when they want to (although there is a very strong "Save Clayoquot Sound from Logging" movement currently underway which seems to indicate this pristine position may only be on hold)!

Locals consider fishing the "traditional industry" of the area and indeed, most days of the year will find boats unloading catches of crab, cod, shrimp and prawns, scallops and clams, and in summer, salmon. Of all the places along the rugged outer coast of Vancouver Island that *should* have fantastic salmon fishing this region is it. Tragically it is far down my list as a choice for pure fishing adventure. Why mention it in this book? Because it is one of the most scenic and enjoyable destinations on the west coast and because the *potential* for spectacular fly fishing is enormous if the few remaining wild salmonid stocks are allowed to rebuild through tighter regulation and elimination of the local roe-herring fishery.

Like it does with so many other loud minority groups, the Canadian Department of Fisheries and Oceans supported a herring seine fishery here that added very little to the economy while killing untold thousands of young Clayoquot salmon and steelhead each spring as part of their "incidental" catch—and it may even have caused a repressive economic impact on the community when the reduced sports fishery yield is factored. Two years ago the roe-herring fishery dwindled and while herring stocks are still very low, young salmonids are said to be making a strong comeback. That, coupled with the efforts of a local sports group which built, finances and operates a very sophisticated salmon hatchery in cooperation with the DFO, makes a bright picture for the future of salmon in this beautiful place. Support is gladly accepted and donations can be sent to Dick Close, P.O Box 69, Tofino, BC V0R 2Z0 (checks payable to: Salmon Program). This is an exceptional operation and deserving of any and all help.

Still—at least at this stage—people seeking quality saltwater fishing usually end up 25 miles south of here in the village of Ucluelet and the rich waters of Barkley Sound (which we'll cover next). No tantrum this time—just the facts as reported to me by a retired wants-to-remain-anonymous fisheries official who lives in the neighborhood.

TOFINO, B.C.

Right in the heart of Clayoquot Sound is the unique town of Tofino, a favorite haunt of fishermen, photographers and nature lovers and an international summer tourist destination catering to those who come to explore endless miles of remote white-sand beaches, hike and camp in unmarred hills, kayak along the awesome coastline and endless inlets or canoe in isolated rivers and mountain lakes. Some who come just want to enjoy seeing the ocean and its bounty of whales, seals, sea lions, otters and bird life. But while the 1,103 year-round residents welcome outsiders to share their place on the planet, many are also dedicated environmentalists who solidly oppose any efforts to upset the natural surroundings or interrupt their way of life.

Likes attract, and nowhere is it more evident than in Tofino. This place offers all the amenities and services required by any traveler and from early June through Labor Day every available bed, room and all 700 camp sites will be filled. Even with more than a dozen motels and lodges, over two dozen B & B's, and six or seven RV/campgrounds in the area, without a reservation—or unless you know someone who lives there—chances are slim there will be anywhere for you to stay.

The same goes for dock space, it's very limited. Many people bring boats big enough to sleep on, but then can't get space to tie up. So plan ahead and reserve if that describes you (Weigh West Marine Resort has the best facilities). Smaller boats also might have trouble getting a spot during the high season, and calling to reserve space will save the frustration of having to launch and take out each day.

Fishing boat rentals are nearly nonexistent. The only two boats I was able to confirm available for rent (as of August 1994) are at Weigh West Marine Resort. Resorts and lodges have charters (boats with fishing guides) available for guests, but outsiders who don't bring their own boats or reserve a charter will have problems getting out on the water—which may be a blessing in this country. There are myriads of shallow flats and bars, rocks and reefs around that claim boaters—even locals—every year. Those who want to find the best fishing spots will just have to be followers and have good fish-finding instincts, or what is recommended even more—hire a guide for a day or two. Ask to be shown the most productive areas and explain the kind of fishing you want to do and that you will be going on your own after that. Fully equipped, just-show-up charters run about $75.00 per hour, but are worth it. Most charter boats can handle four persons, and six or eight hours on the water is enough for anyone.

Of all the areas we talk about Clayoquot probably has the most potential for good and bad experiences. When salmon are in fishing can be easy and everyone catches fish, and there are so many islands and reefs around you can get away from difficult winds or weather and still have good fishing. But when fog rolls in—and during the best fishing times in July and August fog is a fact of life—those same islands can become a confusing array of barriers. Without local knowledge of water courses to follow and a Loran or GPS guidance system or marine radar you might be stuck for a few hours on any given day. These comments are not meant to scare anyone from coming here, just make them aware of the *potentials* of this place in particular. As with anywhere along the west coast, respect is the maxim that must be adhered to.

COHO ON THE ROCKS

As intimated, this is not the greatest salmon fishing destination around, but there can be decent fishing here. After launching at one of the four sites head north out of the harbor. The big island on your right with its two moody—sometimes misty, sometimes sun-haloed—mountains is Meares. It also contains some of Canada's biggest still-remaining cedar and hemlock trees. Use that as your point of visual reference. Turn left into Duffin Passage and follow the buoys towards Wickaninnish Island, then head south out Templar Channel (the numerous small floats you will pass mark crab pots. These are no-nos). A couple of miles along at the entrance is Lennard Island and a fog signal, and outside are reefs over which water heaves and crashes big time! Keeps you alert. There are usually fish around here in July and August and well worth a try as long as you keep your ocean-senses about you and learn a few things about fishing reefs.

A few years ago I watched a fellow fly fishing along a kelp bed uncomfortably close against the wash rocks. He was basketball player-tall, tanned and fit and dressed in a heavy sweat shirt and shorts. An upside-down pipe was tightly clenched, and his baseball cap was on backwards revealing long blond hair. He peered intently at his target from the front of a short, beat-up, low-water Whaler knockoff. A big black lab, paws set firmly on the bow-rub balanced right at his side also watching. Together they made the boat look top heavy and very unstable as it rocked with the swells in this wild water.

The surge would pull them in towards certain disaster then just before the boat returned with the backwash he would cast casually and perfectly right at the edge of the kelp and strip out line like mad, then hold the line tight. The moving boat pulled his fly through the froth and bubbles as effectively as a fast strip and no doubt with far more action.

On about the third or fourth cast he connected with a coho that jumped high, ripped completely around his boat and headed out towards me, jumping stiffly the whole way—a solid fish. He played it like a pro and quickly got it to his boat where I thought his lab was going to do a Kodiak bear thing. It didn't and I was pleased to watch him release the fish. He looked up, waved, and motioned me over.

Keeping my eye on the reef I got as close as I dared and noticed from his "CF" boat registration that he was from California. No wonder he was fishing in such a precarious manner. The guy was in California bliss, no doubt a child of "the Valley" (having lived in California while in university I easily identified the type), totally oblivious to the seething danger.

"Looks like you're doin' all right. I've never had the guts to ride the surge like that," I tried not to sound too patronizing.

"Yeah, I fish this way down in Monterey and up around Point Reyes for sea trout, salmon—anything that's there. I've been coming here and to Ucluelet every year for about ten years—since before the highway was paved." Oops, that made him more than just the naive guy I had him pegged to be.

"What do you do?"

"I'm a fashion photographer in San Francisco. This (he held out his fly rod) is my only passion in life and the only way I can completely unwind."

Fashion photographer naturally meant beautiful women, skimpy swim suits, see-through lingerie, *Playboy*, Frederick's of Hollywood, Victoria's Secret, etc., right? It turned out he does male fashions, and later, after getting stabilized together on a bottle of Teachers blend, I learned he was gay. He's a tremendous individual and we have been close fishing friends ever since.

"How did you turn-on to this method of fishing around reefs? It honestly scares the hell out of me to be this close in?"

"Well, you always want kelp between you and the rocks. I also used to always keep my motor running because I thought I might need it to get away quickly...but it's happened so rarely I usually don't bother anymore. The worse thing is you get pushed into the kelp, but your boat will stick there. Sometimes the backwash is strong and you get caught between it and the next surge—and *that* can get exciting! And you could get minced if a breaker rolls over on you, so you do have to keep half an eye out. But it's sure where the fish are. I lose a few to the kelp, but it's worth it."

As we talked and fished together over the next few days I got more comfortable with this new method. I learned to cast into the outwash, give some line to let the undercurrent pull the line deep, and then let the motion of the boat move my fly. Then after two or three surges go by, a quick strip to get ready for another cast. It was fast fishing to say the least and hits could come any time, but usually it was when your fly started moving up through the churning water.

My friend uses a full extra fast type IV or V sinking line, 9-foot leader plus tippet, and 25-pound-test monofilament backing. His casts rarely went over 50- or 60-feet. I still prefer my shooting taper and running line which I feel cuts the water a little better because of its smaller diameter. After fishing with him over several years now I believe my system allows better line control and that he misses a few strikes because of more slack. In the first few sessions on this trip that wasn't the case, however.

Early one afternoon on a rare fogless day we traveled down past Cox Beach and Portland Point to fish the reefs out from Schooner Cove Campground at the north end of Long Beach. The surface was calm and swells weren't too bad but in towards shore we could see and hear the surf as it pounded against the shallows on the low tide. There were several dozen boats and every one looked to be hauling in salmon—trollers, moochers, jiggers—it didn't seem to matter. Typical west coast salmon fishing! Certainly.

Gulls and diving birds—always a clue to where bait is—were in feeding mode as we pulled up next to a house-size kelp bed at the point of a long reef. This day we lined up and let the surge push us along parallel to it. Casting ahead of the drifting boat gave the same effect as being in a backwash and allowed our lines to sink deep and stay in the water for an extended time as we drifted. It didn't take long. My friend nailed a spectacular 12 pound coho on the first strip. It took me three casts. And it was like that for the next four hours. Every reef and rock wash contained salmon that day, not unusual for this stretch when the run is in and you can get down here from Tofino. There is often good coho action all the way along clear to the entrance of Barkley Sound—about 18 miles south, and the same distance north to Kutcous Point on Flores Island. The entire stretch is prime, clean coho water—shallow, kelpy, reefy—and if bait is around fish can be found anywhere. The only down side—if it can be termed that—is that there are also thousands of redtail, striped, and white sea perch in the sandy areas, and greenling, rockfish, and small lings around the kelp beds that will all readily take flies, and some chew hard enough to shred them so take a bunch.

Interestingly, all the flies my friend uses are conventional ties. Long hooks like size 4 2X, with silver tinsel around the shank, a few strands of polar-white hair on the belly, and sparse pea-green and chocolate or blue hair over, and a built-up head with yellow eyes. The finished fly is about three inches long. They were deadly over the three days we fished together—even out-fished my Firecrackers—though some of his success was no doubt due to retrieve technique. He was able to focus completely on the program at hand, while I am always gawking at the scenery or thinking about where to go next.

At the end of the week my friend headed back to San Francisco and I stayed, anxious to try his methods in some different water—on Chinooks.

BROWN WATER CHINOOK

I'll start this segment off by admitting that sometimes Chinook salmon are the most elusive critters that swim! Even when you can see them they don't always bite. And when that trait occurs in a region where springs aren't too plentiful to begin with...well, it can be downright frustrating. You only get so many opportunities on any given trip.

Outside the entrance to Father Charles Channel (I wish I knew the history of the name), is one of the best places around Clayoquot for Chinook. The top ten- or 12-feet of surface water out here is sometimes a brownish-red color in July and August, a soup of planktons and zooplanktons pulled from the vast backwater shallows of the Sound by the outflow. The dense richness attracts shrimp and baitfish which in turn attract predator fish. Dave Stewart, ex-commercial fisherman and long-time outdoor writer in BC, says unequivocally, "Brown water is spring salmon water." (This assumes we're not sitting off the estuary of some river that is pumping out mud). I have known about so-called "brown" water for a long time and have occasionally experienced great fishing along seams where it mixes with clean.

Another phenomenon that occurs along the west coast is "blue" water. This is the crystal-clear, warm, tropical water carried along by the Japanese Current. Normally it stays from 30 to 100 miles out, but it sometimes moves right in near shore during July and August and displaces the cold, green BC coastal water for a time. It also brings an interesting array of warm water aquatic species—sharks, sea turtles, mackerel, bonito, albacore tuna, sunfish... If you can find the seam where blue water and cold coastal waters meet, it can also produce exciting salmon fishing at times.

In August 1983 when El Niño began affecting the west coast, blue water moved right onto Vancouver Island's outer shoreline. Salmon fishing was not productive except in certain specific spots such as deep holes over which the warmer water formed an inversion, trapping colder water below or on squid spawning beds where salmon went to feed.

One morning I (literally) ran over a huge sunfish in the bay on the outside of Spring Island at Kyuquot. It was the most grotesque creature I had ever seen, all body and fins, big eyes, and a little flimsy tail. For a lark I decided to try and snag it on the head with my fly and take a picture, but it went down before I could get ready. My friend Tim Tullis from Peachland, BC and I tried to do the same thing with a 20-foot whale shark we nearly ran over in Rincon de Guayabitos, Mexico one year, but it too sounded before we could hook it. What a great picture either of these would have made...(sick mind).

That same summer of 1983 in Kyuquot, the group of guys I was with from Vernon, BC all caught mackerel while trolling for salmon (these voracious critters from southern waters will feed on any baitfish or other fish—including young salmon—they can get in their mouths), and in Kyuquot Harbour we heard about an 11-foot hammerhead shark that was shot and killed right under the government dock where children were swimming. Scary stuff.

Anyway, back to Father Charles Channel. It was about 7 a.m. and boats were congregated in two or three tight bunches close to Wilf Rock in the area known as Glory Hole, fishing a rising tide. The water was murky, but not the soupy brown water I described earlier. Still, feed was plentiful and a few springs were being caught.

I watched the action for awhile before nosing into a kelp bed near an elderly couple mooching live herring. Their boat was tied to a bulb and their long, limber rods were in holders bobbing gently with the flat swells.

"How's fishing this morning?" "We got one," the man offered. "*I* got one," the woman corrected. I decided they were probably man and wife. "Lots'a bait around and there's been a few jumpin', but we sure can't seem to hook 'em." " I got *two* nice ones yesterday," again the woman.

The man slumped a bit lower in his seat, fiddled with his radio and then folded his arms over an ample paunch. "Sounds like there's some weather comin' later this week. Got this here portable 99-band, 800-channel, 66-watter that tells me what it's doin' in China or Florida any time of the day or night." I was sure that was valuable information to have out here. Whew.

Because I was inside the rocks the surge wasn't strong enough to carry me into the kelp and back out, so I just cast down along the fronds instead of trying my new-found technique. On about my tenth cast I got a soft hit but it didn't hold on. Bait was everywhere and a spring about 20 pounds sauntered by under my boat. I cast in the direction it had gone but there was no interest.

"Do ya' catch many fish that way?" the man asked. "Uh, yeah, I do all right. Probably not as well on springs as you do using bait, but enough to keep it fun." Just then two more, both in the same 20 pound range, torpedoed by ignoring my fly. Obviously they were moving on live feed. "Damn, why don't they hit?" I muttered. "Two nice springs heading over towards you folks."

"We're ready." The lady picked her rod out of the holder in anticipation. After a couple of minutes she put it back and I caught a snide "Well, where are they?" look as she bent over and busied herself with something on the floor of the boat. A few minutes later—and this is the truth—I could hear a sizzling sound and the smell of bacon drifted across the water, followed awhile later by the odor of burning toast. Then the Mr. was chowing on a toasted bacon sandwich. I was thinking, "Now would be a great time for a bite." No pun intended (I crack myself up sometimes).

I kept casting and retrieving. After nearly an hour I was comatose. My arm was dead and my mind totally separated from my body. Of course, *the* hit came just as I was streaking from Jupiter to Venus.

My stand-in body reacted about fifteen seconds after the Chinook had jumped and thrown the hook. "Shi...oot," I spluttered, remembering the lady next door. "Missed him." I had been thinking about leaving, and now, feeling uncomfortable at not being able to openly discuss my state of mind with the fish I had just missed, my decision was made. I waved to Ma and Pa Kettle as I moved away.

I headed north along the outside of the numerous reefs of the La Croix Group islets, idled past Tree Island and down into Ahous Bay on the outside of Vargas, and slowly explored the reefs inside Blunden Island. I stopped and cast at promising spots, and the few boats I passed didn't show any more signs of action than I got. Nothing was going on. The fog had retreated and looked to be well beyond the horizon. The sea was still flat as I turned east and headed around the northern end of Vargas. At the far end of Brabant Channel I ran into "brown" water flowing out from Calmus Passage. A very high tide had come and gone and the seam was unmistakable in the mini-rip formed by the ebbing flow over Coomes Bank. Diving birds were working the edge coming up with needlefish about three inches long. "All right, let's see if Mr. Spring Salmon is home."

Before I could get unwrapped to cast, there was a slosh right next to my boat. Bait spurted out of the water, and a Chinook arched after them. Another one rolled further out. "Man oh man, easy meat."

A dozen casts later, with fish crashing all around me, I still hadn't had a hit. "*What* am I doing wrong?" I tied on another Firecracker and cast. Still nothing. I changed to a floating line and a weighted pink Polar Shrimp and ripped it across the surface. One boiled on it but didn't take. "That's more like it!" Thirty more minutes of futility and I put my rod down. "What's going on here?" I wondered out loud.

Breaking out my old herring rake (an ancient legacy of my blood-and-guts days) I started up, drove ahead and combed the rusted teeth into the bait school. It impaled two wiggling needlefish. I dumped them on the floor and studied them. Three inches long, light olive-green backs, silver sides, white bellies—perfect match to my Firecrackers. "So what gives?" Plain and simple: salmon don't always eat the patterns you present to them no matter how closely they match the real thing. Probably a smell thing. I picked up the baitfish and tossed them over the side then stroked the fly between my fingers.

Motoring back to the bait, I cast right into the thick of it and let my line sink for several seconds to get below the school where springs usually hang out. I stripped slowly, Chinook-style. Nothing. And there was nothing on the next 20 casts either. After that the school moved on with the tide, the frenzy died, and I slumped against my console. I really felt bummed out. "Hey, don't be such a whimp—that's fishin'!" Never mind. I could see scotch on the menu and some "feel sorry for myself" fishing notes as I slowly motored back to Tofino along the shallow back route.

At 5:30 the next morning it was foggy-cold as a friend and I put on our waders and sneaked down to Cox Beach at low tide to dig razor clams— something I hadn't done for eons. The process is to find a clam hole in the sand, drive a shovel blade in beside it and quickly pry out a scoop, then drop to your knees and dig like hell with one hand. Razor clams can themselves dig down almost as fast as you can and sometimes you end up almost to your arm pit by the time you get your hand under it and pop it out. We played for over an hour and finally ended up with about a dozen nice ones.

While preparing them for breakfast it occurred to me that the exceptionally high and low tides that week were probably part of the reason for the poor Chinook bite. Extreme tides seem to effect them more than coho. Even so, there would be at least one tide during the 24 hours that shouldn't bother them too much—probably the second low of the day at about 3:30 that afternoon. I had quit before low slack the previous day and may have missed the "real" feeding period. But now it was time to feed me. We dipped the clams in a milk and egg mix, rolled them in crushed crackers and fried them quickly in a hot pan. Served with the scrambled egg/milk mix and a succulent smattering of crab meat, it was a grand breakfast—typical west coast fodder.

I headed out at noon without a set plan on where to go. I still wanted to try my new-found surge technique on springs so I headed back to the heavy water reefs and kelp beds on the seaward side of Wilf Rock at the entrance to Father Charles Channel. Most of the morning Chinook fleet had already gone in by the time I got there and I had my pick of spots.

I chose a reef with a break all the way through it and kelp on both sides. Bait would move back and forth depending on the tide. The surge was long and washed far up the sloping rocks before sliding back down. I got ready and motored into position, not quite as confident alone as I had been with my friend. I kept the motor running.

The first few casts were ineffective. My boat didn't have the right momentum and the line wouldn't pull with the backwash. I watched the water for a minute and determined the best backslide was where the rock face was a little steeper. The water came off faster and pooled deeper. Repositioned, I started over. Much better. I hooked four rockfish, a greenling and a giant sculpin in as many casts. At least there was action.

Suddenly, baitfish crowded under my boat and salmon were everywhere. Coho. I quickly had two strikes and didn't hook either one—too slow on the uptake. "Slow down, James, concentrate on what you're trying to do." My next cast was perfect. I fed line, let it sink, then gripped the running line loosely as the boat slid back swimming my fly.

The strike was a quick smack. I lifted the rod expecting a black rockfish and instead line peeled out of my baby bathtub. When it hit the reel I pointed the rod straight at the departing fish. When the run stopped I snapped the rod up two or three times to set the hook, and the fish ripped off again, this time on a good long run. Not being comfortable close to the rock wash I put my engine in gear and steered out towards open water. Twenty minutes later I netted a still lively 20 pound spring a half-mile from where I started. It swam fiercely away the second I let it go. "All right, Jim! One more time..."

As I headed back towards the reef one of the big party boats from Ucluelet was just nosing into my spot. What a production *this* was. The boat looked about 60- or 70-feet long and rolled sluggishly with the swells. I counted 17 people crowded around the railings all hanging on for dear life with one hand and waving fishing rods with the other. We call these boats "pukers" for the obvious reason. Two deck hands were running around baiting hooks and tossing out lines. People at the bow were literally right on top of the kelp and snags would be inescapable. If several salmon were hooked at the same time it was going to be the proverbial Chinese fire drill. I decided to tie up to the kelp a little ways away to watch what developed.

It was a short wait. The bait handlers chummed the water with buckets of dead herring and paraded back and forth among their charges like platoon sergeants along the front line. Soon there was shouting and excitement on the far side of the boat, then two rods bucked in their holders at the same instant on my side. Then a third reel buzzed. Watching the guests trying to pry the rods out of the holders while being thrown around as the boat dipped and rolled was fun enough, but when one lady just started reeling in her fish with the rod still in place, I died laughing. Pictures for sure, and I took a few (though I've never used them I run across them now and then and have a good chuckle).

One hot Chinook streaked right under my boat, did a U-bender around a kelp stem, headed back to the surface and hopped *over* my kelp-tied bow rope. The fisherman must have been using about 30-pound-test because that poor fish came to a quick halt. "Hey, mister could you get my fish untangled?" Distressed voice. A boy about 12.

"No, but I'll sure be happy to net it for you. It's just struggling here." "OK, great! Thanks." Politeness counts.

I netted the fish, about an eight pound spring, and freed the boy's line. He was excited and thankful when I turned it over to him, but I couldn't help but wonder what being on a meat boat might do to his understanding of what this was all about. I realize the majority who go out on party boats are just plain good people enjoying an outing away from maddening city life somewhere and this is their big opportunity to be on a boat and experience fishing for the first time and see fabulous ocean and sea life in a natural setting. They have as much right to this as I do and their memory of the experience—good or bad—will last a lifetime. Mine tend to become merely better or worse events from which I attempt to extract knowledge and wisdom and then judge the value of the experience based on that rather than just accepting each as a new and fresh occurrence. I envy the tourists their simplicity of acceptance.

CLOSE ENCOUNTERS

My most recent trip to Tofino was the first week of August 1994 to update information for this project. Bob Jones and Dave Lornie accompanied me, Bob as photographer and Dave as a fellow fly fisher to try some ideas and a few new patterns. We stayed at the home of Dick Close, owner of Weigh West

Marine Resort. Dick, along with his significant-other, Holly Baker, are avid salmon fishers and are very interested in developing a fly fishing clientele. Both made their boats, time, and local knowledge available to us which proved to be very valuable.

Our first day was spent in the usual familiarization mode. Under a bright, clear sky and no wind we spent time at several of Dick's favorite spots. One was Tree Island, a jumble of rocks and kelp reefs and a small islet with a stand of trees. Only one other boat was there but they quickly reported via radio that they had landed three Chinooks, the largest about 35 pounds.

Dave and I looked at each other and moved in near a wash rock surrounded by kelp. A deep channel open at both ends ran along the kelp. It was high slack tide, bait was below the boat, and three springs had been caught in the past hour so fish were there. The setting was perfect.

I put on a weighted squid pattern with 8-pound tippet and Dave went with a new Mylar pattern he wanted to try. Bob and Holly stationed her boat for photographs as Dave and I went to work casting up-current and letting our flies go deep. On the third or fourth cast as my fly drifted up from the bottom on the retrieve I got a familiar tap-tap and quickly set the hook. A heavy fish flashed and bucked just below me for a moment then straightened out and ran about 100-feet directly at Holly's boat, wallowed on top, then headed deep. I pumped it back and it came easily but headed into the kelp as soon as it saw the boat. Dave backed us out into more open water, and in a few more minutes after a couple of short lunges it was at the boat—a bright 22 or 23 pound spring.

"Piece of cake," someone said, an elucidation which proved to be the Kiss of Death. What looked like the beginning of spectacular fishing—after all this was our first morning and probably only the first couple of dozen casts— ended with a few photographs and the release of that fish. While I did hook two more springs that same day, and Dave landed a nice coho the next morning while we were surge fishing near Portland Point, it was the only salmon I caught in Tofino waters in 1994 which added further—though perhaps unfair—credence to my earlier comments about this area not being as productive as some others.

Dick and Holly did everything they could to dispel my disposition about Tofino fishing. Over the next five days we fished every rockpile, kelp bed, reef, island and bank they knew that had ever contained fish. We saw spectacular sights and witnessed trollers unloading limits of big coho and Chinook taken in deep water every day. We even tried out in the deep a couple of times, but the final score was fly fishers *zip* and meat fishers 10. I suppose I caused those nice people to squirm a bit, but in truth, I just didn't have it on that particular trip. If fish had been in, everyone would have caught fish, including Dave and I. It would truly have been "A piece of cake." But no fish in the areas where we concentrated separated the men from the boys. I sure don't blame *my* inconsistencies on Dick and Holly. In fact, two days after I was there my friend Doug and his wife Nancy went over at my urging and cleaned up on coho and Chinook using Zzingers. Go figure!

Stories that Chinook had entered Barkley Sound were making the rounds when we got back to Tofino Harbour on the final evening, so I decided to spend the last three days of my allotted time down in Ucluelet. Tofino had been tough.

GETTING THERE—TOFINO AND UCLUELET

BC Provincial Highway 4, also known as the Long Beach Road and Pacific Rim Highway, splits off BC 19, the Island Highway, just outside Parksville. It's about 30 miles over to Port Alberni. From there it's just under 60 miles to the junction. Five miles to the left is Ucluelet, and right about 20 miles takes you to Tofino. The road is paved all the way and well maintained, but it is quite winding in some parts so plan on two hours from Alberni whether or not you are pulling a boat.

Our old standby, the "Accommodation and Travel Guide" available from BC Ministry of Tourism, Parliament Buildings, Victoria, B.C. V8V 1X4 lists motels, lodges, campgrounds and services in both towns, and I recommend very strongly that anyone contemplating a trip to this region obtain one and secure accommodations long before heading there. You can also receive information on Barkley Sound and the other two units of Pacific Rim National Park from Superintendent, Pacific Rim National Park, Box 280, Ucluelet, B.C. V0R 3A0, and additional local information is available from Travel-Infocentre, Tofino, B.C. V0R 2Z0—Phone 604/725-3414.

For those interested in family programs, there are several here. Local air services can fly you to a remote lake for a day or three of trout fishing, or steelheading in-season, for a nominal cost. Boats or canoes and primitive accommodations are also available through this service. They will also drop you off on one of many isolated clean, white-sand beaches in an area where you can hike and beachcomb and fly cast from shore to your hearts content, and there are outfitters who will arrange everything for a stay in the Broken Group Islands.

As mentioned, there are very few rental boats available and these are often reserved. If you bring your own boat, launching is no problem, and fuel is readily available, albeit expensive, but dock space can be a problem. There are several boat charter services and sources for tackle, guides, maps, charts, etc., but as previously suggested, bring all the fly gear you think you'll need and clothing to cover every weather extreme. Those of you who are familiar with outer coast fishing will know what I mean. It can be warm and balmy inshore, but a day out on the open ocean can be bone-chilling.

Equipment needs have been pretty-well covered within the text. Boaters, obtain charts 3640, Clayoquot Sound and 3671, Barkley Sound.

BARKLEY SOUND

This is not necessarily a case of having saved the best for last, but Barkley Sound might easily qualify for that. Roughly 20 miles across and extending almost the same distance inland, these rich waters teem with salmon and bottomfish, baitfish, squid, vast flocks of resident and migratory sea birds, and a myriad of other critters including otters, harbor seals, California and stellar sea lions, and gray whales. Every trip I make here discloses some new wonder not previously encountered or noted. I suspect one could spend a lifetime in Barkley Sound and not experience all there is.

Spackled with an uncountable number of islands, islets, reefs and rocks, and containing the Broken Group Islands Unit of Pacific Rim National Park, Barkley waters are reached from three areas: Ucluelet at the top northwest entrance to the sound, Bamfield at the lower southeast entrance, and Port Alberni way at the back to the northeast. Traveling by boat from the latter means a long trip down Alberni Inlet to decent fishing (about twice as far as the run from Gold River down Muchalat Inlet to Friendly Cove in Nootka Sound), but if you have not secured motel or campground accommodations in the two closer towns or are not prepared to camp in primitive surroundings (i.e., on an island), this may be your only alternative. Load up on fuel and start early.

Much of Barkley Sound qualifies as "protected waters," especially along the Bamfield (southeast) side where the Deer Islands form a long barrier against the open sea and the Imperial Eagle Channel with its wide open strait. Here, Chinook and coho fishing are subject to more usual seasonal runs as they pass through Hammond Passage and Trevor Channel on their way to spawning waters up Alberni Inlet. Fly fishing can be good on this side, but you have to be there during the few days or weeks when a run comes through or you'll be doing a lot of sightseeing. More on Bamfield waters later.

The northern end of the Sound is quite different with big open water, deep holes, scattered islands, reefs and kelp beds. The main shoreline here is protected from prevailing winds, but out in the Sound it can get nasty. This water has good fishing virtually all year long, and jumps to excellent in springtime and early summer from just inside the entrance clear out towards the Continental Shelf in the wide open ocean.

The Broken Group Islands are in the center of the Sound. Nearly 100 islands covering 30 square miles make up this unit of the Pacific Rim National Park reached only by boat. There are a number of primitive campsites here if you are so inclined (information on writing to the Park in previous "Getting There" section). Summertime fishing can be fantastic as coho swarm around nearly every point and Chinooks drift up from ledges 100-feet below to feed on baitfish right at the surface and in the kelp.

We'll describe all three areas and the best times I've found to be there. Right now I'm so excited just thinking about it I don't know where to begin...

UCLUELET, B.C.

Down the road about 25 miles from Tofino and tucked into the northwest corner of Barkley Sound is Ucluelet, a fishing-destination village of about 2,300. While it is said that Campbell River is "The Salmon Capital of the World" by virtue of the highest annual average catch per boat per day, Ucluelet (pronounced you-clue-let) can be said to have the most consistent all-year salmon fishing on Vancouver Island. Hold on to something as you read this next part. It is the only place I would stick my neck out and say, "You won't fail here if you can get out on the water!" While it *is* seasonal with weather and times of the year making success less or more certain, there are always fish in these waters. Given time, good hunters just won't miss. The reason is Barkley Sound and its perpetual and abundant supply of herring, needlefish, squid and at times, anchovy.

Where Tofino is a "something for everyone" sort of place, Ucluelet is more of a pure fishing destination. That's not to say anyone coming here won't find what they are looking for. It has its share of awesome seascapes—rugged shorelines and clean white beaches, surf ripping over reefs and sending waves a mile high, wind-swept trees next to shore, mountains... Out on the horizon the ever-present fog bank backdrops a bright blue ocean, sea birds of every kind, migrating gray whales and passing ships. Hiking and picnics, kayaking, exploring inside the calm waters of Ucluelet Inlet, wonderful rose-colored summer evenings...

South of town through the trees are three municipal beaches—Big Beach, Little Beach and Terrace Beach—the latter reached by a boardwalk trail through He-Tin-Kis Park. Farther south on the peninsula the rocky shoreline provides great hiking—albeit rugged—and sometimes spectacular fishing. For anyone who likes to cast from shore with a good possibility of hooking a salmon, rockfish or perch, the rock points, channels and reefs in this area are excellent. The entire coast here is littered with kelp and baitfish, and if the waves aren't too wild it provides a great challenge. It's all there. But the fishing...oh, man!

Like Tofino, Ucluelet is usually full throughout the summer months and often in May and September. You'll have a tough time finding room even to camp. And whatever you do, don't just drive there planning to park along a side road or in town. It won't happen. Plan and secure rooms or RV/camp space at least several months before you go.

CHINOOK AND COHO WATER

As I have stated once or twice so far, I'm a great one for not heeding my own advice. When I landed in Ucluelet after a week in Tofino, I didn't have reservations anywhere, and hadn't checked ahead. Everyone in town must have called friends and relatives to tell them the Chinooks had come to shore because there was barely even a parking spot! Needless to say, I called my friend in Tofino to tell him I'd be back that evening and not to change the sheets. I ended up launching and unlaunching and commuting 50 miles round trip each day for the next three days. A pain, but it worked out.

After leaving the harbor and traveling down through the entrance to Ucluelet Inlet, then rounding Amphritrite Point and the Coast Guard Station and light house there you'll be in some of the most prolific salmon water any-where. From here for about five miles up the coast to Florencia Island is an extremely reefy and rock-studded section with deep bays, channels and inlets that contain good numbers of resident Chinook and coho. And in August when migrating salmon follow baitfish in from the offshore banks, the entire area comes alive with fish. This is one of those "you can't miss" deals I was talking about. Trouble is, it's tough to target a specific species. They're all mixed together and just when you think you're going to nail the big spring that you've cast to, a coho peels in and takes the fly. Tough, tough to take.

In June and July the best fishing is offshore from a couple of miles out to more than 20 over what are called the "banks." There are several underwater ridges and shoals out there that rise to within 100- to 200-feet of the surface and hold heavy concentrations of bait. It's primarily an open water troll fishery 40- to 60-feet down, but on several occasions I have seen bait, birds and salmon literally as far as the eye could see on the surface, and have hooked fish—big fish—until I was tired. When you hit it like that—which is *not* out of the ordinary here—you'll swear it's better than sex (at least at my age you might).

Trouble is, this is big-time, big-water with all the potential hazards the west coast can assemble. And without experience and intimate knowledge of the area, the banks are difficult to find. You can just head for the boats you'll see far off on the horizon, or travel with the fleet that heads that way every morning, and you'll get there all right. The problems occur when fog rolls in, sometimes between you and shore while you're still in bright sunlight; or a fast moving storm runs you down; or a harsh offshore wind catches you napping; or boat trouble, etc., and you can't get home. Even near shore around here good navigational skills are an absolute must.

Short fog got me story: One July in the years before I bought a Loran unit I was fishing the "bite" about 10 miles out at what is locally called "the wreck." It had been a clean night—no fog—and in the morning the sky was clear and sunny (watch out when it's like that). I left with the crowd but part way there I found an acre of boiling herring, gulls in a frenzy above and salmon below. I hooked a really nice Chinook in only a few casts that pulled out line far into my backing, and for the next half hour I was busy working it. I noticed boats going past me heading in but didn't pay much attention until a cold, chilling breeze swept over me from behind. I looked back and fog was rolling at me only a hundred yards away.

If I didn't start immediately I was going to be enveloped. I glanced at shore and got my bearings, then read my compass, certain I could get in. I didn't want to give up the spring I had on. But that didn't last long. Within minutes I was socked-in and a state of angst overcame me. I heaved on the fish and tried to horse it towards the boat. Nothing doing. I pointed my rod, broke it off, cranked my engine and aimed at the last spot I had seen daylight. I never found it.

For the first time in my boating life I had to slow down and rely one hundred percent on my compass. I motored towards shore for awhile until a new thought occurred: All this was going to do was get me close to shore, in among the reefs and wash rocks. I wasn't familiar enough with the landmarks around Amphitrite Point at the entrance to Ucluelet Inlet to know when to turn. I'm not afraid to admit it was frightening and I had to constantly fight the panic that rushed over me in waves! But I continued on, figuring I'd face whatever obstacles when I came to them.

The first sign I was close to shore was the sound of the fog horn off to my right and the sound of surf pounding over a reef. I couldn't see rocks but I could almost feel them. I turned right and drove for about five minutes. I had almost reached the height of major anxiety when I heard the drone of a diesel close by. I shut off my engine, closed my eyes and pointed at the sound. When I blinked open my arm was pointing almost straight ahead, so I ran quickly in that direction until I crossed a heavy wake and turned with it.

Half an hour later I was safely in the harbor, which was just in the edge of the fog bank but at least I could see which direction to go. The boat I had followed was a big commercial seiner, and I stopped to thank the captain. "Had you on my radar all the way in. Glad I could help." Me too!

I've said it several times so far, don't mess with Mother Ocean. If you are not prepared to handle such emergencies as the one I went through by yourself, then don't get in that situation. It's damn scary.

BAMFIELD

As mentioned earlier, some of the best fishing in Barkley Sound occurs on the Bamfield side, especially throughout August. But unlike Ucluelet waters, Bamfield fishing is more dependent on annual runs moving up Trevor and Imperial Eagle Channels, and when they do fishing can be spectacular.

Except for one quick stop recently it's been over ten years since I spent any time in Bamfield. Canadian friends who still go there every year for the Chinook fishing say nothing much has changed. The town—village—itself is the northern demarcation of the West Coast Trail Unit of Pacific Rim National Park, a 48 mile trail along the Pacific ocean from Port Renfrew to Bamfield. Before the turn of the century there were so many ships wrecking along this stretch that a permanent trail was built to aid in rescuing survivors. Today, this rugged trail is recommended for only the most experienced hikers (for information contact the Pacific Rim National Park at the address in previous "Getting There").

Located about 60 miles (allow at least two hours driving time) south and west from Port Alberni over a well-traveled logging road network, Bamfield has managed to maintain its character as a west coast fishing village better than most. Separated by Bamfield Inlet and edged by a network of waterways and boardwalks, residents here are more at home in boats than cars. On the east side of the bay (at road's end) are a full-service campground, boat launch, a couple of restaurants and motels, government docks and a commercial fish plant, while across the inlet in West Bamfield are the general store, various docks and stores, a small first aid clinic, walkways, etc.

Along both sides of the inlet heading out to open water are homes, B & B's, a native lodge, fishing guide services, fuel stations, the Canadian Coast Guard, and unusually friendly people. Stay around here for any length of time and your comfort-zone will increase ten-fold!

When salmon run everyone gets in on the action. Around the points at the entrance to the inlet I have seen women and children in small boats hauling in salmon on handlines, guys "trolling" in one-man rafts, guide boats, canoes. Farther out, among the islands and reefs of the Deer Islands, and southwest towards Cape Beale trollers will be working the hot spots. In the early years I guess I fished all the best places.

CHINOOKS DOWN AND DIRTY

My last time in Bamfield was the fourth week of July, 1993 when my friend Doug and I made the long run down Alberni Inlet in the early dawn hours, cut south across the channel at Tzartus Island and went in to Bamfield for breakfast and fuel (for those interested my OMC 100 hp outboard burned ten gallons one-way. I'm not known as a pussy-footer). We were told there was an early run of Chinooks out in the reefs at the Cape and off Boat Rock across the channel.

Fog blanketed the entire entrance as we approached the open ocean off Cape Beale. I wasn't familiar enough with water out there to chance going in blind, so we stopped at Whittlestone Point to wait for it to lift. I've had excellent fishing for coho here but—for me at least—it's never been the "sure thing" for springs as some other areas. Doug and I were both sort of in our own fog as we tied to kelp at the base of a steep wash rock and let the boat drift back with the outwash. In the distance the fog horn on Cape Beale was bleating its message across the sound, and several boats were working sandy Tapaltos Bay just out from us, a good spot for halibut earlier in the year. If bait was around, it also produced springs.

We poured coffee and set up to string our rods. Doug wanted to try a brand new 11-foot Shimano mooching rod and single-action reel that he bought for fishing along the Oregon coast so he rigged for strip-casting with a two-ounce crescent weight, bead chain, and a nine-foot 17-pound-test straight monofilament leader. Gentle lobs with this outfit produced 100-foot casts! He hooked up a Firecracker and was in business before I even had my rod out of its case.

To be safe Doug aimed his first cast out the back of the boat towards the long, sloping sand shelf of the bay. The water was only about 30-feet here and his fly was on the bottom almost immediately. Two strips and he got a smashing strike. The fish took line immediately and we both figured it was a spring. Once on the reel it was a horse, ripping out line in short spurts that had been gained a few inches at a time and hammering the long, limber rod almost uncontrollably. With rod tip bent all the way to the water he slowly gained line until a shape loomed and a chick-halibut about 18 or 20 pounds flapped to the surface.

I took a slurp of coffee and needled him. "Man, if that puny little halibut gave you that much trouble, you're *really* gonna have your hands full with a big spring." Little did we know.

In the next hour we landed another small halibut, two small lings, a couple of kelp greenling, and I had lost a big heavy "something." But no salmon. Finally, the fog lifted enough that we could see the reefs and rocks around King Edward Island and we headed across Trevor Channel.

Two commercial Indian fishermen were just bringing in a Chinook on the outside of Boat Rock as we went by. Theirs was the only boat there and they told us they had taken several springs up to 30-pounds that morning. I wondered at their navigational skills. I had some pretty sophisticated electronic gear on-board and *I* didn't chance the fog. These guys were in an old open fiberglass outboard without so much as a compass and had been here for several hours.

The drift that morning was south to north along the face of the rock. Both of us cast ahead of the boat, let our flies go down about 40-feet and then walked the lines to the back. As we drifted through a school of bait my line lifted and I stripped in to cast again. With the 2-ounce weight Doug's fly stayed down and just as it started to lift he hooked up.

At first the fish stayed deep and just bucked and we weren't sure what it was. All we could tell was it was heavy. Then Doug hammered the hook home a couple times and Mr. Chinook hit overdrive. Line screeched from the little mooching reel until it stretched almost flat across the water about 75- or 80-

yards. The big spring wallowed on the surface, turned and sounded. Doug reeled as fast as he could against slack line and finally caught up with it back at about the same area where it had hit. Obviously the fish had returned to the school. Then it was a pump and reel program. Three times it came to the surface nearby only to rip off again. At last it seemed ready to come to the net and as Doug lifted his rod I stabbed the net towards the fish (*big* mistake as all good netters know. Let the fisherguy lead the fish to the net). It spooked, dove straight down in a mad rush and Doug's brand new graphite mooching rod exploded at the ferrule with a crack that sounded like a rifle blast.

"What happened?" an incredulous tone from my friend Doug.

"I'm not sure. Did your rod hit the railing?"

"No, it just collapsed when the fish went. Man, that was a great fish, too, what...about 30 pounds?"

"Yeah, probably." I really felt guilty about the rod. I knew what had happened but I wondered if Doug did. "That was my fault, you know! I got excited and poked the net out at him when I should have waited."

"The rod still shouldn't have broken." (The upshot of the story is, Doug later returned the rod to the sporting goods store where he bought it and it was replaced).

After the trauma of losing the fish wore off, Doug set up one of my fly outfits and we went back and found the bait school. Over the next two hours and several passes we hooked two more springs in the 25 to 28 pound range, typical size for the runs of this area which are nearly all hatchery or SEP fish. We nodded to our native fishing partners—who were still hauling in fish—as we left.

COHO THE EASY WAY

It was past noon as we headed northeast along King Edward Island and Diana Island, vaguely in the direction of Port Alberni. At Kirby Point—on the Imperial Eagle side of Diana Island—the swells were washing far up the steep slope and back down, forming a near-waterfall into the kelp bed there. No boats were around, but there was a lot of bait and a good chance salmon would be in the neighborhood. I decided to show Doug how to fish the wash.

Spooked at first, we both finally settled down and fished the kelp on opposite sides of the boat. It worked as usual. Cast out, give some line, hold on for a minute to let the boat pull the fly, then strip. Whammo! We both hooked coho almost at the same instant. Mine went east (into the kelp) and Doug's somersaulted its way into clean water, a hot little fish about six pounds.

We stayed until it wasn't a challenge any longer, and moved to new country for me, a big sandy bay on the north side of the long island just above Tzartus. There is a great kelp bed there and the water was sparkling clear. A breeze pushed us east along the shoreline and we stripped our flies as we drifted along. We caught coho after coho in water less than 20-feet deep, all in the same size range of six to eight pounds.

At Tzartus Island we went through an opening back into Trevor Channel and stopped to fish a likely-looking kelp bed at the exit. I hooked a rockfish and released it and as we drifted away it was still on the surface. Suddenly a bald eagle launched out of a snag on shore, dove towards the water, and snatched the quivering rockfish in a low pass only 30-feet away. There were two more sitting on the highest branches and thinking it was a good photo-op, we went back in and caught two more rockfish, stunned them and threw them out and got our cameras ready. I can't say much for our photography but the eagles sure didn't disappoint.

As we left I felt satisfied the country is still spectacular, pleased that the scenery hasn't changed all that much in the 26 years I've been coming here. There is more logging, of course, and I saw a few more houses and lodges, and a hell of a lot more boats than I remember, but it's still OK and I highly recommend boating and fishing around this area.

An hour later we turned the last corner of Alberni Inlet heading towards the pulp mill and ran into a fleet of over forty seiners there for a three-hour sockeye salmon opening. Our way was completely blocked by nets and we spent the next couple of late afternoon hours sitting next to a DFO Zodiac chatting to government personnel who were overseeing the netting operation. An interesting conversation that I won't bore you with other than to say as far as they are concerned "that (all the seiners) is what it's all about!"

BROKEN GROUP CHINOOK

The last couple of years in early August excellent runs of Chinook have shown up around the shoals near the entrance to Ucluelet Inlet and in the better-known spots near Bamfield that we just talked about, and anyone who could get out generally caught fish. Always ask locally where the fish are and the answer will often be "Right outside." There are fantastic reefs on both sides and anywhere bait can be found will almost surely produce fish.

But for year-after-year consistency the Broken Group can't be topped. Any time from late July through August and into early September runs of coho and

Chinook move continuously through the islands and shoals and linger to feed before heading for home rivers up Alberni way.

I earned my Chinook badge here a number of years ago on the outer edge of the Broken Group near Cree Island. That first year I boated from Bamfield. It's about the same distance as from Ucluelet, but can be tougher because of the wide expanse of open water across Imperial Eagle Channel into prevailing swells from the west. From either direction it's a healthy trip, but the fish are here and early August seems to be *the* time for the biggest fish of the year.

My last trip was in 1994, at the tail end of the two week trip to Tofino and Ucluelet described earlier. The runs had moved into Barkley Sound following the bait schools and I launched at Ucluelet Harbour at the gentlemanly hour of 10:00 a.m. to catch the early afternoon high tide. I was heading for the Broken Group and some familiar water. It was breezy and since the fog didn't seem to be a threat I took my time and explored some of the islands and reefs on the way. Every kelp bed I stopped at yielded coho, and several times I ran across large bait schools in the open water of Loudoun Channel. If I didn't see salmon I didn't stop, otherwise I would never have made it to the islands.

The Broken Group terrain is awesome, there's no other way to describe it. Everywhere are jagged reefs and rocks, pristine treed islands, bays and inlets, kelp, kelp, and more kelp, sea birds, sea lion colonies, whales. It's a world unto itself.

The outer islands of the Group temper the water from the full force of the sea, and inside can be delightful. There is danger of being lulled into a state of contentment that suddenly turns to dismay when it's realized the wind has come up outside or fog has covered the way home, so it pays to keep in touch with what's going on. I speak from experience. On my second-ever trip out there I spent a long, lonely, cold night in my 15-foot aluminum boat, anchored in a small bay and bundled up in life jackets to stay warm because I was afraid of crossing the Imperial Channel in a heavy wind. That was in the days before I knew enough to carry extra water and food, and a sleeping bag when I went exploring. It was also before I had a VHF marine transceiver and couldn't contact anyone to tell them where I was. The upside was the guys I was with in Bamfield knew I could take care of myself and figured out what I'd done when they saw the wind. The downside is I've done it a couple of times now and if I really was in trouble, it would take some time before anyone would come looking.

Shoals here are quite shallow and hold good quantities of small baitfish in the kelp. Schools of large herring are often encountered in open water moving towards several of the bays at the back of the Sound where they will stay until they spawn the following March and April. These are adults and they attract big salmon. Squid are also present throughout the Sound, and in spring and summer the lights of Ucluelet Harbour attract them to the docks where people jig them. Must be an interesting life being on everyone's menu.

From previous visits to the Broken Group I had found a long underwater shelf that rises straight up from about 60-feet off the ocean floor to 12-feet beneath the surface at low tide. I have intercepted springs as they moved from the deeper water to feed right along the edge of the drop-off and at times right up on the shallow flats. Because of the depth, trollers rarely get in this far so I usually have the "hole" all to myself. There are many such places throughout the islands here and careful study of a nautical chart will reveal them. Just look for a deep channel or shelf that ends against a rising shoal, then drift or tie up to kelp or anchor in the shallows and fish along the sides and out over the drop-off. I suspect bait moves along these same corridors and the salmon follow, fulfilling an ancient symbiotic relationship.

Outside Cree Island is a spot I particularly like. A notch of deep water intrudes several hundred feet into a shallow bench and has a flushing action with every tide. There are enormous numbers of bottomfish in and along it, but there are also Chinooks. I pulled in and tied up, pleased to see the kelp beds were still healthy. I sat for awhile just breathing-in the clean air, listening to the sea birds chirp and beep and hearing the deep coughing grunts of a California sea lion colony a mile away. What a place. Blue sky, bright sun, a few clouds sticking to the tops of the Mackenzie Range mountains off to the northeast. Thoughts of the deck that needed painting, lawns that were growing knee-high, and the garden that the weeds would be taking over—all were a thousand miles away. I couldn't imagine being anywhere else.

I shook off the contentment and checked on the fog bank. It was at least ten miles out and the breeze had flattened. A hundred yards off to my right a school of herring dimpled the surface and it was less than an hour to high slack tide. Everything was perfect.

I made a few casts along the kelp and true to form caught two quillback rockfish and an 18-inch lingcod that destroyed my Firecracker. The herring were moving my way and I thought I saw a swirl. I re-armed with a new fly and waited until the school was about 100-feet away then fired it towards them. Two foot-long strips and I got a hit. Missed. Missed again. It was just pecking at the fly, something probably wasn't quite right. My next cast went about 40-feet and ended in a tangle. I sorted it out, put the rod under my arm and stripped with both hands to get it in quickly so I could make a decent cast. On about the fifth or sixth stroke a spring absolutely crushed the fast moving target, immediately went ballistic and threw the fly. It wasn't big, probably ten or 12 pounds, but it surprised me a fish could hit that hard and not get hooked.

The bait school was next to my boat now and I cast to the far side, let the lead-core sink the fly for about ten seconds, and again started my slow one-foot-long Chinook strips. Nothing. And nothing on the next several casts either. Then a big boil about 30-feet in front of my boat as a spring arched out chasing a herring that was skipping across the surface to get away. My line was in the other direction and with my eye on the chase I again stripped in with both hands. Halfway through a pull my line came to a solid stop, went slack and an instant later a chunky Chinook charged right by my boat trailing orange running line. It was going full steam and just before it hit the reel I raised the rod to cushion the shock and started the reel spool moving by stripping out line (believe me, I don't always think quickly enough to do that but it helps prevent break-offs). Fifty-yards melted off in nothing flat. Finally the fish stopped and settled down to a normal Chinook power struggle.

It came to the boat in fairly quick time—probably too full of herring to do much fighting—and when it rolled on its side I gave slack and the fly fell out. I righted it, it gasped a few times and then slowly swam out of my grip.

I sat there a minute thinking about what had just happened: "Those guys hit when I was stripping with both hands. They must want it fast today?" (I love talking to myself, the logic of my conversation always amazes me). After checking the leader, my next cast was as long as I could make it. Thirty seconds count, then a long quick retrieve stroke. A few casts later, another missed strike. Two or three casts after that a coho nailed it and sailed into the air. A half-dozen cartwheels and it just quit. I reeled it in and saw that it was gushing blood from the right gill plate. The fly was firmly hooked there and had ripped a gill, so I quickly killed it and scheduled it for Dick's barby that night.

The tide was slack now and 100-yards across the channel I could see a commotion on the surface. I motored over to the spot where several small rhinoceros auklets were popping to the surface with four-inch needlefish in their short bills. My sounder showed a large bait school about 42-feet below and though I couldn't see any large fish on the screen, I was sure they were there.

Somewhere along the way I had ordered a dozen Sand Lance patterns from Orvis. I loop-tied one onto my 12-pound-test tippet and cast. As mentioned earlier, loop-tying allows the fly to move freely giving it better action—especially important with long-tailed flies like this one. The lead-core sank for about one minute before I tightened, got in touch with the fly and started my usual slow big-salmon retrieve. Between strips I paused to let the fly descend, the long tail fluttering downward. On the strip it would tilt up and move in a swimming motion.

I stayed with the bait school and on about my fifth cast I got a crunching strike 40-feet below. At first I had a flush of disappointment, it didn't feel like a spring. But when my line zipped straight away and backing peeled off the reel and I felt the great exultation of an adrenaline-charge, I knew this is what it's all about!

As I had done countless times before, I became focused. All bad things melted away. The world elsewhere was still going along, but out here in the open sea among the islands, reefs, birds and other life, with a fish on, I was totally involved in the age-old struggle of man and nature—one on one. Sometimes you meld with it all, become it and the purity of it becomes the reality of everything. Nothing else matters. This great feeling—this ecstasy— is what brings me back to the open sea, again and again.

That, the love of my family, and a few good friends who understand me...what more can a guy ask from life? Well, maybe a sip or two of good scotch now and then.

LAST SHOT

I've always believed in the philosophy that I could have anything I wanted if I wanted it badly enough. When I was younger instead of going along with the crowd I often went the other way (i.e., not smoking or doing drugs when many of my friends were). Rather than reacting to an event as others did, I usually tried to find out what caused it (i.e., watching as my college peers demonstrated in the 60s and trying to understand why). I'm certainly not trying to imply I'm better than anyone—I've shown the fallacy of that by exposing the tiny frauds I commit against the "purity" of flyfishing within the pages of this book! But I have always tried to be true to myself and to act properly for the proper reasons.

I also believe that every individual, company, and even whole industries must continually bear total accountability for their actions and judgments, good or bad. For my efforts I've been called everything from a maverick to a contrarian, and while a vice president in the Fortune 500 corporate world, my labels were sometimes worse than that: When I fired individuals who weren't doing their jobs I was branded a "Terminator." When I dared to make others be responsible for their own mistakes rather than covering for them I was designated a non-team player.

In the grand scheme of things, my philosophy, my efforts, my trials of life—none of these were major plays to anyone but me. So why discuss them in a book about salmon? Because I believe it helps explain what we all sometimes face. There are many of us out here who *feel* what is right and just, and who act every day on what we trust and believe. But much as we might want it to happen, very few of us are ever in a position to truly influence the big picture or induce others to participate in even some part of it.

Even so, I've tried to hold on to the belief that wrong things *will* get better, that bureaucrats and people in industry who control them *will* see the light, that the planet *will* mend itself if we give it a chance. But I'm beginning to suspect there's a crack in my armor. I feel negativism crawling around under my skin, and I'm wondering, does anyone out there *really* have enough facts to allow us to believe in a bright future?

The original title of this book was *Salmon Ecstacy And Remorse*. I think the ecstasy part comes through loud and clear, that there is pure rapture in the pursuit of salmon on their own wild turf (surf?). The power and beauty of it is everywhere out on the open sea, and anyone who seeks it can still find it. Simple! But then things of beauty usually are.

The remorse is the persistent, unerring, progressive decline in the salmonid fishery. Those who understand the ecstasy know this to be true. They also know the itinerary and course are controlled by powers far stronger than each of us.

I read how the logging industry "finally realizes the importance of protecting spawning habitat and is cleaning up its act." Then I hike to a recently-pristine hillside only to find ripped and scarred ground, broken trees, smashed brush, and gouged and muddied streams and bottomland from a new clear-cut.

I hear bureaucrats proclaim, "The salmonid fishery is better off than ever and some stocks are again totally self-sustaining." Then they pay themselves even higher salaries and reduce the amounts spent on habitat enhancement, enforcement and management programs.

We the people are said to be the *power* of government. In control. But then everyone truly understands *that* paradox. We could be in command if enough of us stood up against elected officials who are too weak to chastise poor logging practices, sloppy mining, over-fishing, dams, industrial and agricultural pollution, our own pollution. But we won't. We jump up at meetings and beat our mighty little chests and shout for change, write a few letters to castigate "those bureaucratic bastards in charge" and then the next day call our brokers and give them a buy order for shares in the hottest new mining venture, or have a load of lumber delivered so we can add to the deck, or buy chemicals to spray on the roses or put in the pool, or...

Hey, I've been there and I've done it, and the reason I don't use "I" and "my" in place of "we" and "our" in the above malediction is because I don't know anyone who is truly willing to give up any piece of the comfort zone they have established. Hell no, we've *earned* it.

It's so easy to *proclaim* "If we are to have salmon and other anadromous fish in our future we must act now."

It's a lot tougher to *do* it!